Alain Laboile, photographer
lives in a house alongside a brook with his wife and six children.
His work has gained international success for many years. His
photographs—some of which are award-winning—are exhibited all
around the world. The photographs found in this book have been
achieved with the playful participation of his two daughters, Dune and Nil.

HifuMiyo, illustrator
was born in Hiroshima and has lived in Lyon, France, since 2010.
She works for the international and French press. Her first children's
book was published by Thierry Magnier Editions in 2019.

I Can Do That!

1000 ways to become independent

PHOTOS BY ALAIN LABOILE

ILLUSTRATED BY HIFUMIYO

CONTENTS

In the bathroom
I know how to

In my bedroom
I know how to

At my desk
I know how to

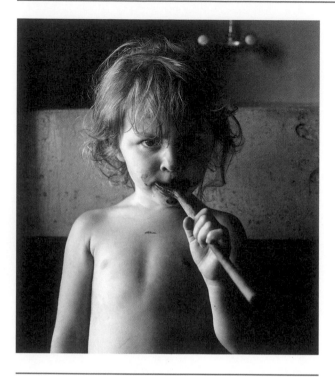

In the kitchen
I know how to

At home
I know how to

Outdoors
I know how to

At school
I know how to

NOTE TO PARENTS

Thank you for picking up this copy of *I Can Do That!* You've taken your first steps toward giving your child the skills they need to become more independent.

Because we know all children are different, we don't want to make the rules about how you use this book. You're the best person to decide whether an activity is appropriate and safe for your child to try out, and that's why you won't find any suggestions about the suitability of the activities for different age ranges and abilities.

However, if you see this symbol:

it means that the activity contains an element of danger—whether that's a slippery surface or a sharp knife—and we strongly recommend understanding the steps involved, checking that it's appropriate for your child, and ensuring they are supervised if necessary.

We also recommend that children have access to safer alternatives— such as safety scissors for cutting—if they are trying activities for the first time or if special adjustments are needed to accommodate allergies and intolerances, such as hypoallergenic adhesive bandages for dressing cuts.

NOTE TO KIDS

Welcome to *I Can Do That*! We're looking forward to teaching you some new skills that you can use at home, at school, and when you're out and about!

Before we start, some of the activities in this book can be dangerous and cause injury. You'll know which ones they are because you'll see this symbol on the page:

If you see this symbol next to an activity you'd like to try, read the page or pages through so you understand the steps, and ask your adult for help.

We all get stuck sometimes. Don't be afraid to **ask your adult** for help if you are trying something for the first time or if you're not quite sure how to do an activity safely.

You might also have allergies and intolerances. If this is the case, check with your adult that the activity is safe for you or whether you need to do it slightly differently.

Now, let's get on with learning new skills and having fun!

In the bathroom

I know how to

I know how to wash myself

Body

1 Adjust the temperature of the water so it is not too hot or cold. Ask your adult if you need help.

2 Lather the soap. Be careful—soap + water = slippery floor!

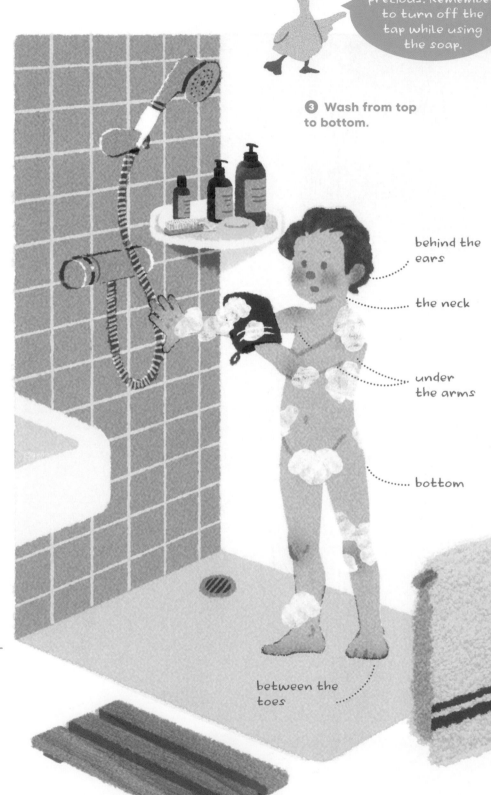

Water is very precious. Remember to turn off the tap while using the soap.

3 Wash from top to bottom.

behind the ears

the neck

under the arms

bottom

between the toes

Hair

4 Rinse yourself from top to bottom.

5 Dry yourself, especially in the folds.

1 Wet your hair.

3 Spread the shampoo all over your hair. Be careful not to get any in your eyes.

5 Rinse your hair well. Remember— keep your eyes closed!

2 Put some shampoo in your hand.

4 Rub in using the tips of your fingers. Don't scratch with your nails.

6 Dry your hair toward the tips.

15

I know how to go to the toilet

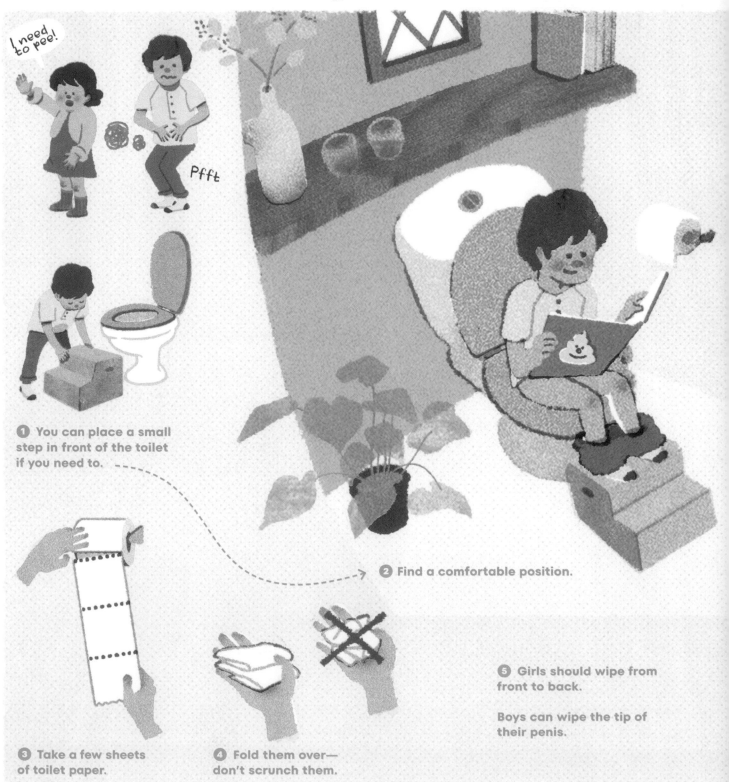

I need to pee!

Pfft

1 You can place a small step in front of the toilet if you need to.

2 Find a comfortable position.

3 Take a few sheets of toilet paper.

4 Fold them over—don't scrunch them.

5 Girls should wipe from front to back.

Boys can wipe the tip of their penis.

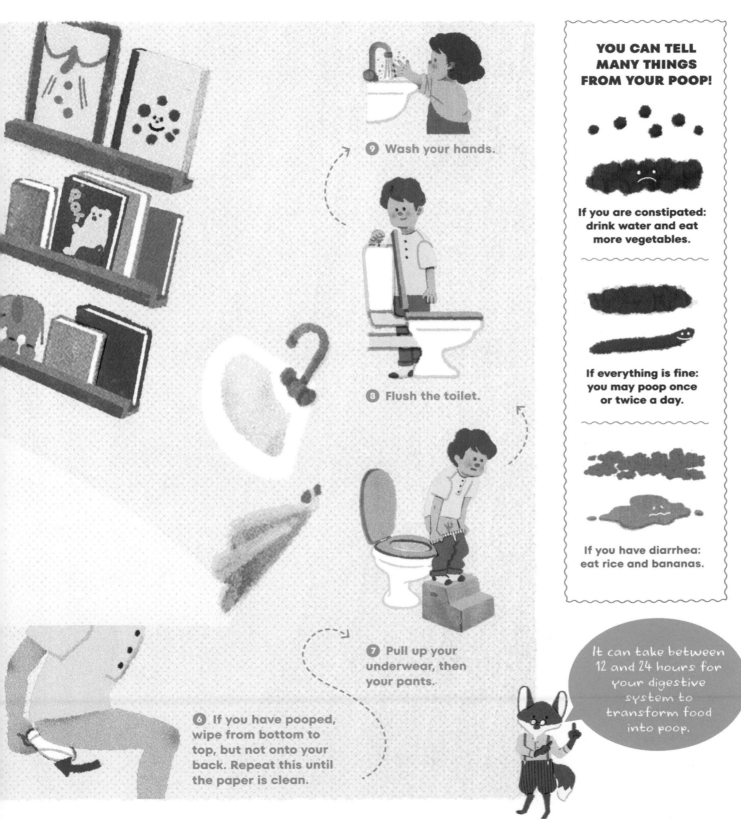

9 Wash your hands.

8 Flush the toilet.

7 Pull up your underwear, then your pants.

6 If you have pooped, wipe from bottom to top, but not onto your back. Repeat this until the paper is clean.

YOU CAN TELL MANY THINGS FROM YOUR POOP!

If you are constipated: drink water and eat more vegetables.

If everything is fine: you may poop once or twice a day.

If you have diarrhea: eat rice and bananas.

It can take between 12 and 24 hours for your digestive system to transform food into poop.

I know how to wash my hands

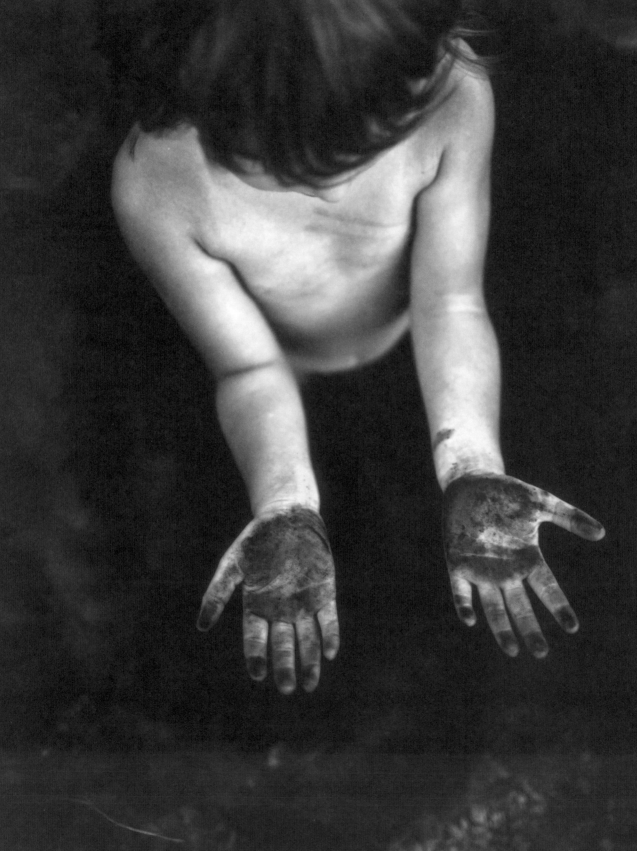

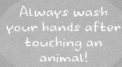

Always wash your hands after touching an animal!

Be careful and make sure the water isn't too hot before you wet your hands. Ask your adult if you need help.

1 Turn on the tap, and let a little water run into your hands.

2 Turn off the tap so that you don't waste any water. Lather up the soap.

3 Rub your hands together to cover them with soap.

4 Cross your fingers to wash in between them.

5 Always wash the backs of your hands, your fingertips, and your wrists.

6 Place your hands under a little running water to rinse them.

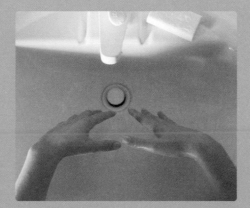

7 Turn off the tap, and shake the water off your hands.

8 Dry your hands with a clean towel.

19

I know how to cut my fingernails

With nail scissors

⚠️ **WARNING!**
This activity can be dangerous and lead to injury. Ask your adult if you need help.

❶ Place the scissors onto your thumbnail.

❷ Carefully follow the curve, and only cut the extra white part of the nail.

 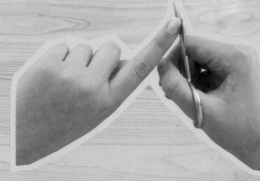

Leave a thin line of the white at the end of the nail.

❸ Be careful not to cut too close to your skin.

❹ Continue with the other fingers. Then, swap hands.

FOR YOUR TOES
Put your heel on the floor, and hold your big toe with one hand. Then cut the nail using the other hand.

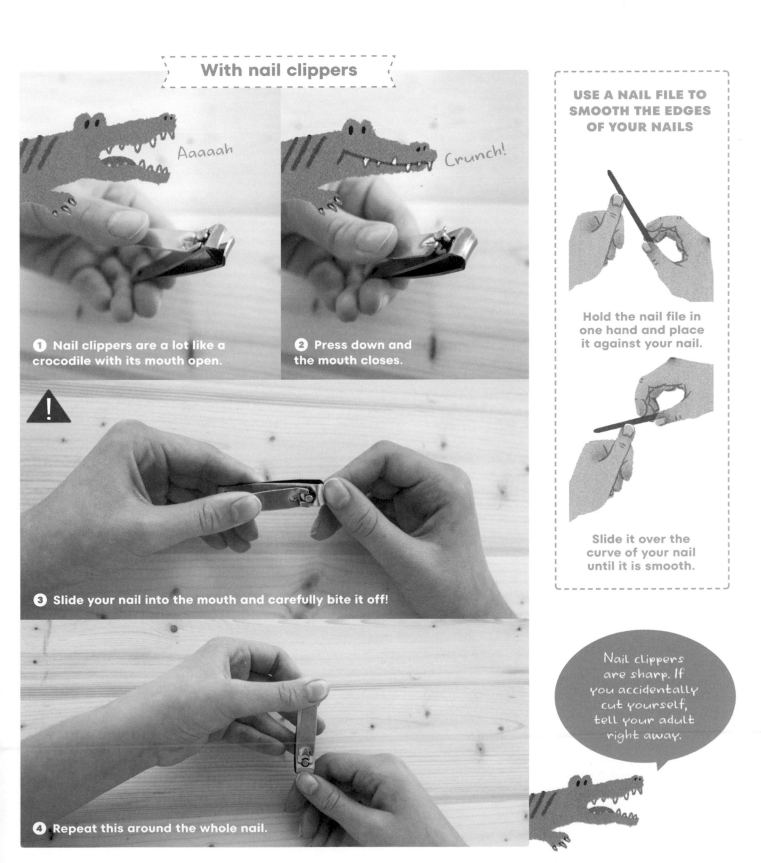

With nail clippers

Aaaaah

Crunch!

1 Nail clippers are a lot like a crocodile with its mouth open.

2 Press down and the mouth closes.

3 Slide your nail into the mouth and carefully bite it off!

4 Repeat this around the whole nail.

USE A NAIL FILE TO SMOOTH THE EDGES OF YOUR NAILS

Hold the nail file in one hand and place it against your nail.

Slide it over the curve of your nail until it is smooth.

Nail clippers are sharp. If you accidentally cut yourself, tell your adult right away.

I know how to brush my teeth

A pea-sized amount of toothpaste is enough.

Squeeze the tube at this end.

It takes about three minutes to brush your teeth—enough time for a little song!

～ How to brush ～

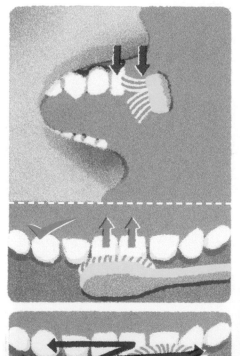

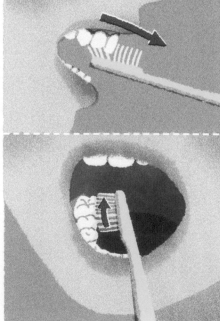

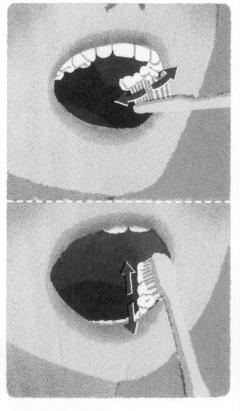

1 OUTER SIDE
Brush the outer side of your teeth from bottom to top and top to bottom, but not zigzag.

2 INSIDE
Brush the inside of your teeth going away from the gum.

3 BACK TEETH
Carefully brush your back teeth both on the top and the bottom.

Replace your toothbrush regularly, especially if the bristles are flattened!

Try to brush your teeth twice a day to protect them from infection.

Yum yum—sugar!

Rinsing

④ Put a little water in your mouth.

⑤ Without swallowing, rinse the water all over your mouth.

⑥ Spit the water out into the sink.

I know how to do my hair

1 Check the water temperature and rinse off the shampoo.

2 Use whatever products are needed for your hair. We all have different hair types, so ask your adult if you're not sure what's best for you.

Brushing

Bring your hair onto one side. Hold it in one hand, then brush through the tips.

When there are no more knots, do one last brush from the roots to the tips.

3 If you need to detangle your hair, it's easier to do this when it's wet. Comb out the tangles little by little, starting at the tips.

4 Leave your hair to dry.

25

I know how to tie a ponytail

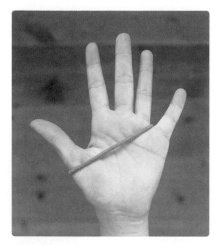

1 Place the elastic around your fingers, except for your little finger.

2 With the same hand the elastic is on, gather your hair and hold it as close to your head as possible.

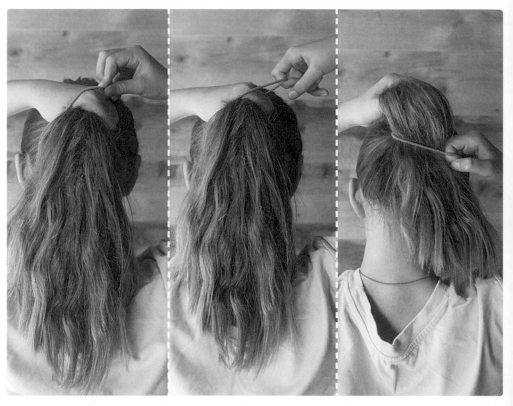

3 With your other hand, grab the elastic and pull the hair through.

4 Pull the elastic and twist it into a figure-8 shape.

5 Put your fingers into the loop of the elastic and grab your hair.

6 Without letting go of your hair, pull on the elastic with your other hand.

7 Once again, pull your hair through the elastic without letting go.

All done!

CLUB DE FILLES
SPRING / SUMMER
2002

27

I know how to attach a hair clip

1 Open the clip and put some hair into it.

2 Slide the clip along your head.

3 Clip it closed!

I know how to do a bun

1 Gather your hair in the same way as you do for a ponytail.

2 Hold it tight, and twist the ponytail around itself with the other hand.

3 Without letting go, continue to twist.

4 You can use your forefinger to twist it nice and tightly.

5 Coil this around the base, like a snail's shell.

6 Place an elastic around your hand and hold onto the bun.

7 Pull the elastic around the bun, just as you did for a ponytail.

Perfect!

I know how to braid my hair

1 With your left hand, pull the middle section under the red section.

2 With your right hand, pull the middle section under the yellow section.

3 With your left hand, pull the middle section under the brown section.

4 With your right hand, pull the middle section under the red section.

Keep going for a longer braid!

Hold onto the end of the braid, and attach an elastic to hold the braid together.

I know how to take care of a cut

Before treating small cuts, let your adult know that you've hurt yourself. Then, wash your hands and prepare everything that you might need.

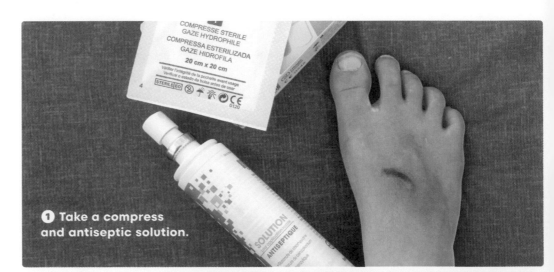

❶ Take a compress and antiseptic solution.

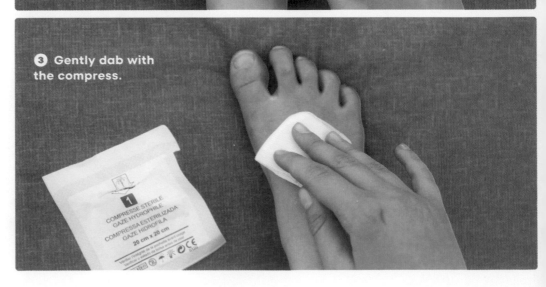

❷ Spray the antiseptic onto your cut. Take care not to get the spray anywhere else.

❸ Gently dab with the compress.

and put on a bandage

Find the right size bandage for your cut.

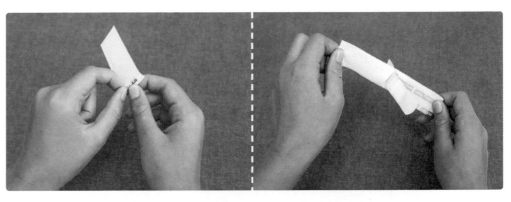

1 Take the adhesive bandage out of its paper wrapping.

2 Peel off one side of the protective paper.

Carefully position the soft part of the bandage onto your cut.

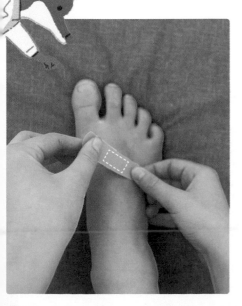

3 Place the bandage over your cut and stick one side down.

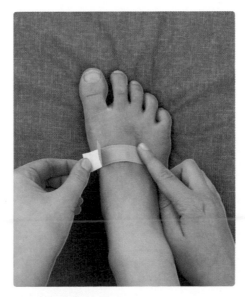

4 Peel off the second protective paper.

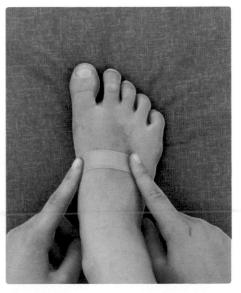

6 Gently press down both sides. All done!

I know how to blow my nose

Don't wipe your nose on your sleeve.

THAT'S DIRTY!

Don't eat your snot.

YUCK!

1 Take a soft paper tissue. Put it onto your nose.

ACHOO!

When you sneeze, put your hand or arm in front of your mouth.

2 Press onto your right nostril. Blow through your other nostril into the tissue.

3 Do the same with the other side.

4 Wipe under your nose.

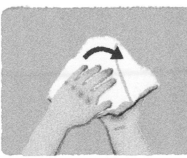

5 Fold up the tissue.

6 Throw it in the trash and wash your hands.

35

In my bedroom

I know how to

I know how to choose my clothes

Even in the summer, it can be cold in the shade or in the evening. Check the weather forecast before getting dressed.

spring/summer

If it's sunny and hot, I choose lighter clothes and sandals.

Sunglasses and a hat will help protect me from the sun.

I choose clothes depending on the day's activity: sports, park, beach, etc.

Ready for sports!

Ready for the beach!

Protected from the rain!

Warm and cozy for snow!

I can even put summer clothes on in winter if I add a sweater and warm tights.

fall/winter

If it's cold, I can wear a sweater and then take it off if I'm too hot.

I wear a hat and a coat depending on the weather: waterproof if it's raining, warm and cozy if it's cold or snowing.

I know how to button my buttons

1 Place the bottom corners next to each other.

2 Put your thumb through the buttonhole.

3 With the other hand, take hold of the first button.

4 Bring the button next to the buttonhole and pull it through.

5 You have done your first button.

6 Continue all the way up to the top!

40

I know how to put on a sweater

1 Place the sweater flat with the back of it toward you. The label will help you know which side is the back.

2 Put your arms into the sleeves until your hands come out.

3 Grab the neck of the sweater.

4 Pull this over your head.

5 Push your head through and then straighten the sweater around your body.

TIP!

Before putting your arms into the sleeves...

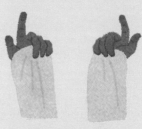

... hold the cuffs with your middle, third, and little finger.

·················· **Taking off a sweater** ··················

1 With one hand, grab the sleeve and pull so you can take out your elbow and then your arm. Do the same on the other side.

2 With both hands, pull the neck of the sweater over your head.

41

I know how to zip up my jacket

1 Slide the zipper down to the bottom.

2 Place the two corners next to each other.

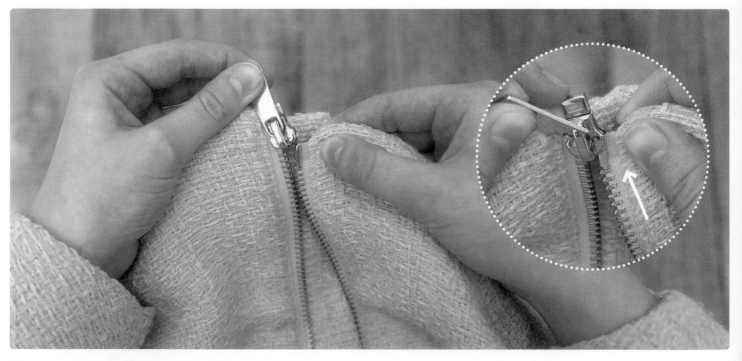

3 Insert the pin all the way into the zipper.

4 Hold the bottom of the zipper between your fingers.

5 Pull the tab upward with your other hand.

And zip!

I know how to put on my coat

Putting on a coat

1 Hold your cuff before you put your arm in.

2 Slide your arm in until your hand comes out at the end.

3 Pull your hood up and bring your coat onto your shoulder.

4 Hold your cuff and put in your second arm.

5 Pull the top of the sleeve toward you until your hand comes out.

6 Fasten up your coat.

TIP!

Taking your coat off and hanging it up

1 With one hand, grab the sleeve.

2 Pull it off your arm.

3 Pull the other sleeve and take your arm out.

4 Hang your coat up by the hood or the inside of the collar.

I know how to put on my socks

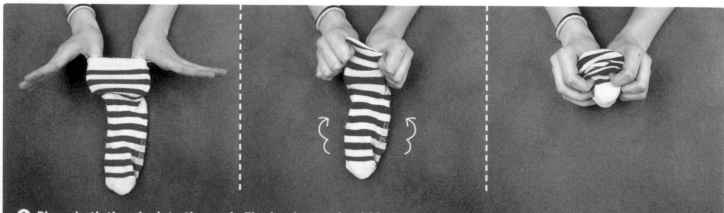

① Place both thumbs into the sock. The heel part should be near to the ground. Then, bunch the sock up with your thumbs.

② Put the tips of your toes into the end of the sock.

③ Unroll the sock over your foot, carefully positioning your heel.

④ Pull the sock up your leg.

If you have pulled it too high, carefully reposition the heel.

I know how to put on tights

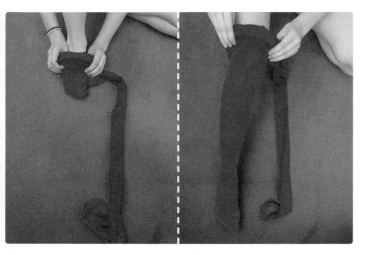

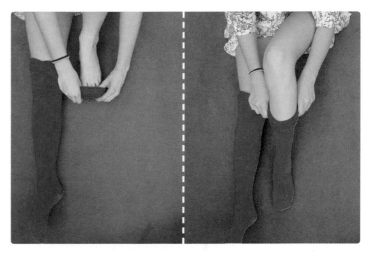

① With your thumbs, bunch up the first leg of the tights and put it onto the tips of your toes. Then, pull to unroll.

② Do the same thing for the other leg.

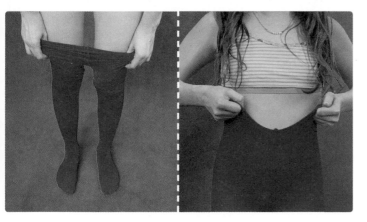

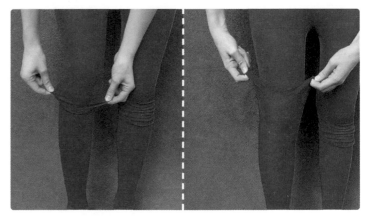

③ Now stand up and pull the tights all the way up to your waist.

④ To straighten them out, use your thumb and finger to pull them straight.

Pull on the boots so you can push your heel in.

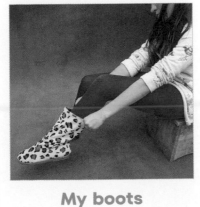

My boots

My flat shoes

Pull the back of the shoe before pushing in the heel.

45

I know how to put on my shoes

I've put my shoes on the wrong feet!

1 Undo your laces. Then, open up your shoe.

2 Pull out the tongue and put your foot into the shoe, toes first.

3 Push your foot inside and press down with your heel while you pull on the back of the shoe.

4 Pull on the tongue and flatten it down onto the top of your foot.

5 Tighten the laces by pulling them close to the holes at the same time.

6 Do this all the way up to the top.

46

I know how to tie my shoelaces

1 Hold a lace in each hand.

2 Cross the white lace over the yellow lace about halfway up.

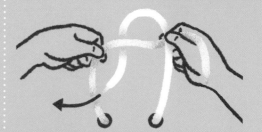

3 Put the end of the white lace under the yellow.

4 Pull both laces until the knot is close to the shoe.

5 Do a loop with the white lace—like a rabbit's ear—leaving a long tail.

6 Do the same thing with the yellow lace.

7 Cross the two ears over in the middle.

8 Bend the top of the yellow ear over the white, and then pass it through the space.

9 Pull both ears until the knot is nice and tight.

Well done!

47

I know how to buckle my belt

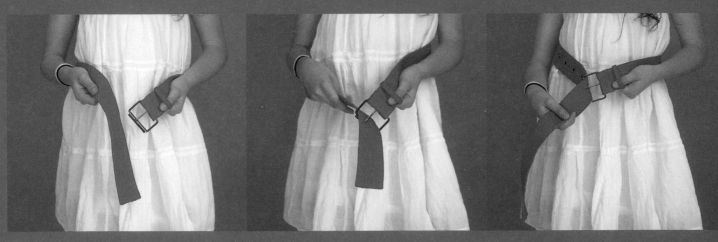

1 Place the belt around your waist, and put the end of the belt through the buckle.

2 Pull the belt—not too tightly!—and push the prong into one of the holes.

3 Put the end of the strap through the buckle and then pull it through the securing loop.

I know how to fasten my watch

1 Place your watch onto your wrist, so you can see the face.

2 Put your arm on a table and turn over the wrist with your watch on it.

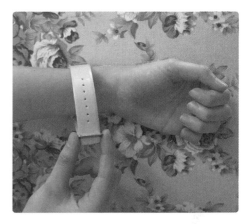

3 With your free hand, put the strap into the buckle.

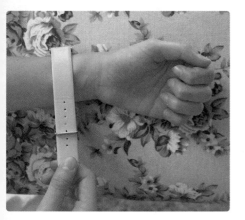

4 Pull on the strap to tighten the buckle around your wrist.

5 Push the prong into a hole.

6 Put the end of the strap through the second part of the buckle and through the securing loop.

My sandals

1 Take hold of the buckle and the sandal strap.

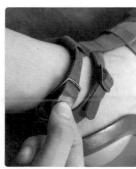

2 Put the strap through the buckle.

3 Pull on the strap to tighten the buckle around your ankle.

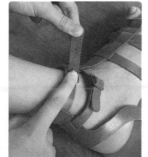

4 Push the prong into the hole.

5 Put the strap through the buckle.

I know how to fold my clothes

Put your arm all the way down the inside of your trouser leg. Grab the hem at the bottom and pull this toward you.

USING A COAT HANGER

Fold your trousers in half over the bar.

A pair of pants

❶ Flatten your pants and fold one leg onto the other.

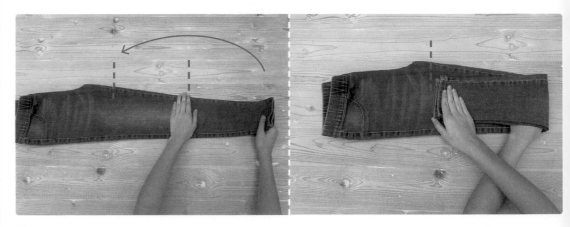

❷ Starting from the bottom, fold part of the leg up.

❸ Fold this in half again. Now your pants are folded into 3!

A sweater or a t-shirt

1 Flatten out your sweater with the back facing you.

2 Fold one side in so that the sleeve reaches the neck.

3 Then fold the sleeve back on itself.

4 Do this same thing for the other side, then take hold of the bottom of the sweater.

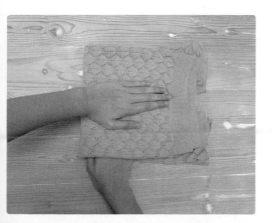

5 Fold the bottom of the sweater over, up to the neck.

6 Now it's ready to be put away with your other sweaters.

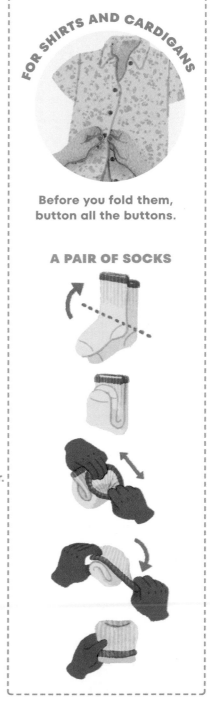

FOR SHIRTS AND CARDIGANS

Before you fold them, button all the buttons.

A PAIR OF SOCKS

51

I know how to go to bed

I know how to straighten up my room

Clothes and shoes

1 I pick up everything that is laying around and make three piles:

clean   dirty   shoes

LAUNDRY

2 I place all of the dirty clothes into the laundry basket.

3 I put away the clean things into the cupboard. I fold clothes to go in the drawer or on the shelf, or hang them on a coat hanger.

4 I put away the shoes where they belong.

Books

1 I pick up all of the books that are on the floor or on my bed.

2 I place them on the bookshelf with the spine of the book facing me.

Oh no!

Toys and paper

1 I pick up all of the toys that are on the floor or on the bed, and I put them into groups: dolls, construction games, cars, felt pens...

2 I then put each toy where it belongs: storage box, toy box, closet...

3 I throw the paper into the trash.

I give back anything that doesn't belong to me to my brother, my sister, or my grown up.

I can also make my bed...

55

I know how to make my bed

Fitted sheet

1 Position the sheet the right way around, paying attention to the short and long sides.

2 Fit each corner of the sheet onto each corner of the mattress.

3 Pull the sheet snugly over the mattress.

Duvet cover

1 Put your arms inside the far corners and bunch it up.

2 Grab two corners from your duvet and slide these into the far corners of the duvet cover.

3 Now grab the corners of the cover along with the corners of the duvet and shake them so that the duvet cover unfurls over the duvet.

4 Once the cover has unfurled all the way down, position this onto your bed and tuck the end of it under the mattress.

Pillowcase

1 Bunch the pillowcase up in the same way as with a sock.

2 Slide the corners of your pillow into the corners of the pillowcase.

3 Then unfurl the case over the pillow.

4 Tuck the last two corners of the pillow into the pillowcase.

57

I know how to pack a bag

For the weekend

- 1 change of clothes:
  pants +
  t-shirt +
  sweater or cardigan
- Pajamas + stuffed
  animal
- Underpants + socks
- Toothbrush
  + toothpaste
- Book

I can write a list so I don't forget anything!

For the swimming pool

- Towel
- Swimsuit/trunks
- Swim cap
- Swimming goggles
- Shower gel
- Comb or brush
- Snack
- A coin for
  the lockers

For school

NOTEBOOK

WORKBOOK

READING

MATH

- Pencil case
- Colored pencils
- Ruler
- Workbooks
- Notebook
- Snack
- Water bottle

I know how to pack a suitcase

1 Make a list of all the things that you need to take. Count the number of days you will be away for so that you know how much you need to take. For example, if you are going away for one week, you will need seven pairs of underwear and seven pairs of socks.

CLOTHES

✔	4	Underwear
✔	4	Pairs of socks
		Skirts/pants
✔	3	T-shirts
		Shorts
✔	2	Jumpers/sweaters/cardigans
✔	1	Raincoat/coat
		Pajamas

SHOES

	Sandals
	Sneakers
	Boots
	Walking shoes
✔	Slippers/flip-flops

ACCESSORIES

	Hat/cap
	Sock hat/scarf
	Sunglasses

TOILETRIES

	Soap
	Shampoo
	Toothbrush and toothpaste
	Hairbrush
	Sunscreen
✔	Towel

FUN

✔	Book
	Stuffed animal
	Notebook + pencil

2 Place your folded clothes into the case, starting with the bigger items that take up the most room. Then fill in the gaps with the smaller items, like socks.

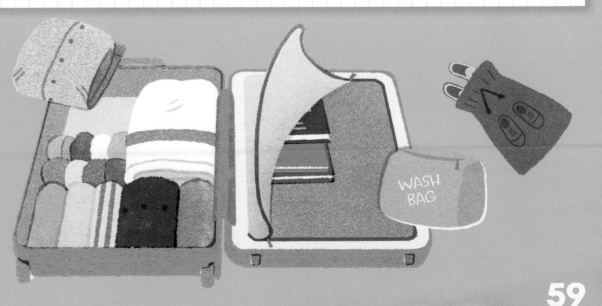

WASH BAG

59

At my desk

I know how to

I know how to organize my things

This is quite messy!

abcd

✗

I'm not sitting properly if...

... the chair is too high.

... the chair is too low.

... I'm balancing on two legs.

Folders to keep things organized

This is a nice and neat desk!

Clear space to work in

A well-lit desk

Pens and pencils in a holder or pencil case

Organized sheets of paper

An emptied trash can

I'm sitting properly when...

... my back is straight and my feet touch the floor.

... I sit on a cushion if the chair is too low.

... I put a step under my feet if they don't touch the floor.

I know how to hold a pencil

1 Open your thumb and forefinger into a "V." Keep your other fingers closed.

2 Position the pencil into the "V."

3 Your forefinger and thumb can then grip the pencil, and you can use your middle finger to steady the pencil.

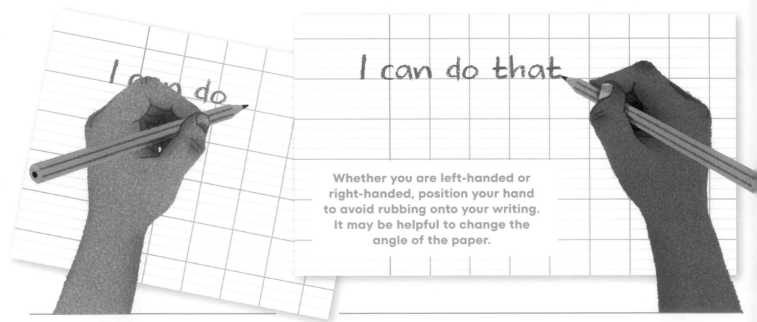

Whether you are left-handed or right-handed, position your hand to avoid rubbing onto your writing. It may be helpful to change the angle of the paper.

Using an eraser

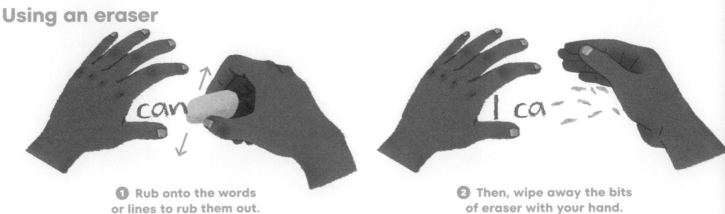

1 Rub onto the words or lines to rub them out.

2 Then, wipe away the bits of eraser with your hand.

I know how to sharpen a pencil

The hand holding the sharpener stays still. The blade is sharp—be careful to keep your fingers away from it.

Use your other hand to twist the pencil in a clockwise direction. Once the pencil has a sharp point, you can stop.

If the sharpened point is too long, it might break easily.

If you use a pencil sharpener with a cap to catch the shavings, don't forget to empty it regularly!

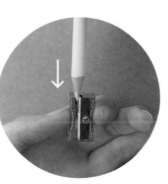

If the tip of the pencil breaks off into the sharpener, push it out with another pencil.

I know how to measure

Understanding the marks on a ruler

The big lines are the centimeters (cm).

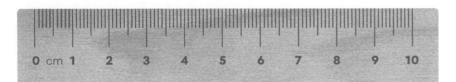

The little lines are the milimeters (mm).

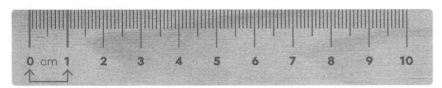

So, in 1 cm there are 10 mm. The line between each number is for 5 mm.

Measuring

1 Place an object on the 0 (zero).

7.7 cm

4.3 cm

2 Then read the number on the ruler.

WITH A HEIGHT CHART...
... to measure how tall you are.

WITH A MEASURING TAPE...
... to measure your waist or head circumference. Put the tape around and read the number under the zero.

DID YOU KNOW?
Feet are not measured in centimeters. A foot measurer will measure your shoe size. For example, a shoe size 12 is equivalent to about 18 cm.

0 1 2 3 4 5 6 7 8 9 10 11 12 13 14 15 16 17 18 19 20

I know how to draw a straight line

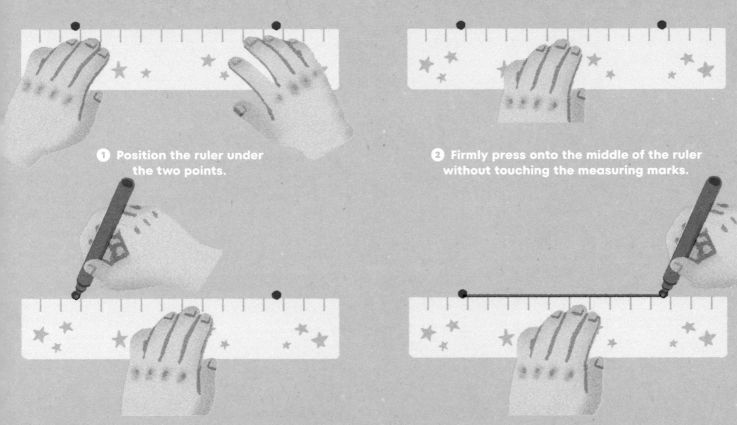

① Position the ruler under the two points.

② Firmly press onto the middle of the ruler without touching the measuring marks.

③ Starting from the left, press your pen against the edge of the ruler and slide it to the right.

If you hold your ruler to the side, it might move.

If your fingers go over the marks, you won't be able to draw the line.

A STRAIGHT LINE TO...

underline

link

cross out

draw

enclose

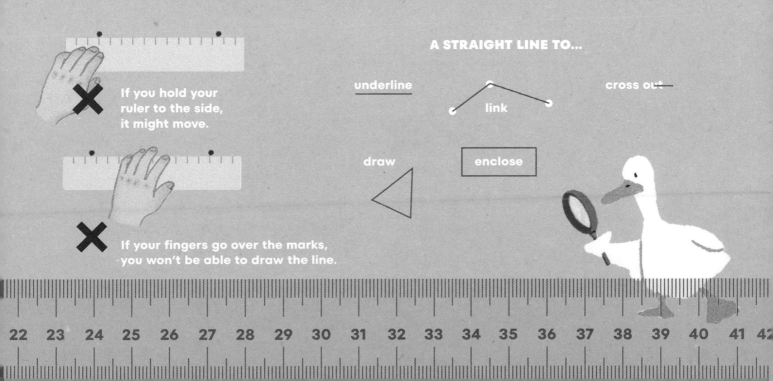

22 23 24 25 26 27 28 29 30 31 32 33 34 35 36 37 38 39 40 41 42

I know how to cut out

Using scissors

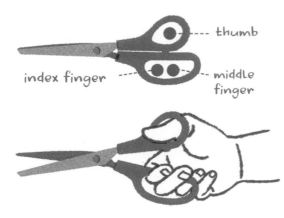

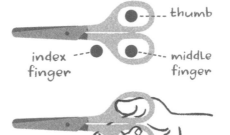

1 Place your fingers correctly, depending on the size of the scissors.

2 Open and close the scissors like a crocodile!

Straight line

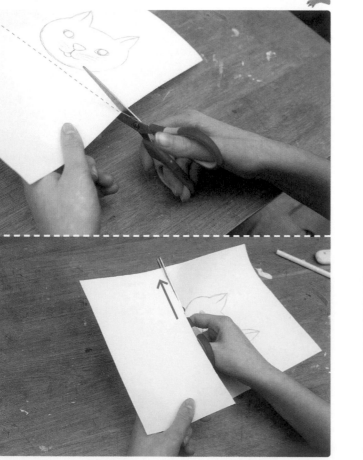

Match up the point of the scissors with the line. Your wrist and arm should be in line with the scissors.

Following a curve

Following the line, turn the paper and your wrist, little by little, as you move forward with the scissors.

By hand

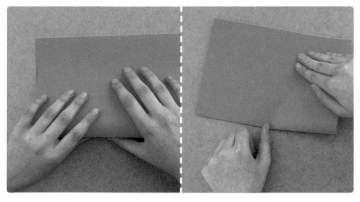

1 Fold the paper and reinforce the fold by pressing along it with your nail.

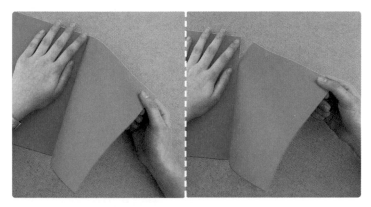

2 Unfold the paper. Press onto one half of the paper as close to the fold as possible. With your other hand, pull the other half away.

With a ruler

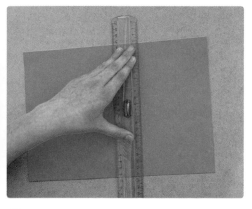

3 Place the edge of the ruler exactly where you are going to tear.

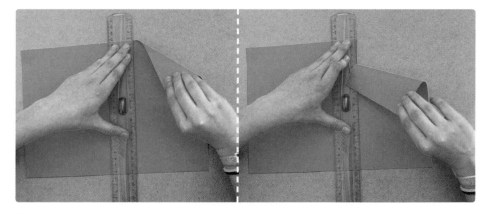

4 Firmly press down onto the ruler and with the other hand, tear the paper away in the direction of the ruler.

REMOVING A CENTER

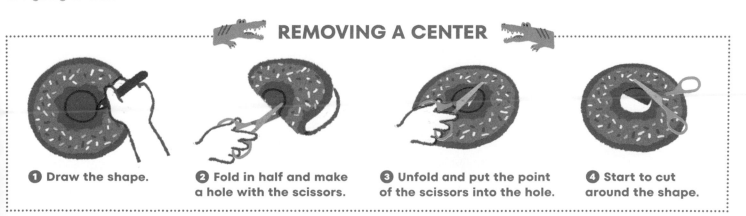

1 Draw the shape.

2 Fold in half and make a hole with the scissors.

3 Unfold and put the point of the scissors into the hole.

4 Start to cut around the shape.

69

I know how to write on the board

Hold the chalk with the tips of your fingers

Lift your hand off the board a little bit to avoid smudging the board.

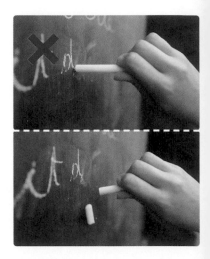

If you hold the chalk at the end, it may break.

If you hold the chalk too straight, the noise is horrible.

Use a dry cloth to erase. If you use a damp sponge, you must wait until the board dries before writing again.

Use the side of the chalk to color in. Avoid smudging with your hand.

A mouse running in the grass.

I know how to color in

❶ Draw a picture

Draw anything you like with a black or colored pencil.

❷ Hold the pencil comfortably

Keep your hand at the bottom of the picture and not over it.

Hold the pencil at an angle.

If you press too hard, it can break.

If you press for too long with a pen, it can make a hole in the paper.

❸ Coloring in

Hold the paper steady with one hand.

Start with the edges.

Finish off by filling it in.

Do quick, short strokes by moving just your fingers.

Don't make sudden gestures with your arm or wrist. This can rip the paper.

Different techniques
Felt pens and colored pencils

Mixing colors
Always start with the lightest color,
then color over with the darker color.

Dots
Add volume by filling your drawing
with different-colored dots.

Shading
By doing crosshatching or
overlaying different colors,
you can create a gradated effect.

From light to dark
For a darker shade, you just have to
press a little harder on the pencil.

I know how to paint

1 Prepare everything you will need.

An old t-shirt or apron

Tubes of paint

Sheets of paper

A cloth

A plate or a palette

A glass of water

Paintbrushes

② Organize your work area. Protect the table with old newspaper or a big piece of cardboard.

③ Gently press on the end of the paint tube to squeeze out a small amount of paint.

④ Dip your brush into a little water, then dip the tip of the brush into the paint without squashing the bristles.

⑤ Always rinse the brush between different colors. Stir it in the water and then drain it on the edge before wiping it on a cloth.

Mixing colors

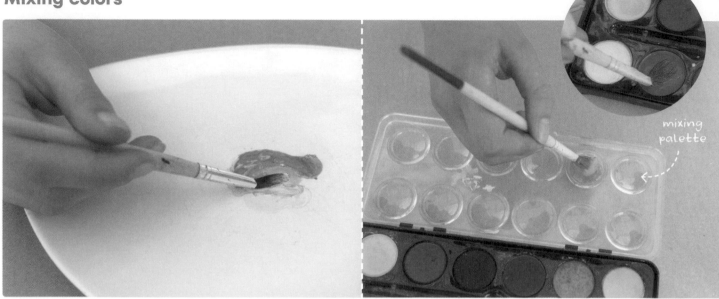

mixing palette

Take a small amount of each of the two colors and put this on the plate or mixing palette.
Mix together until you have created the new color.

TIPS!

Turn your paper to avoid touching the fresh paint.

Put the tops back onto the tubes.

To keep the paints from mixing on the palette, spread them out.

Change the water when it's dirty.

Store the brushes with the bristles upright.

WASHING THE BRUSH

With a small amount of soap, turn the paintbrush in the palm of your hand.

Rinse thoroughly with clean water.

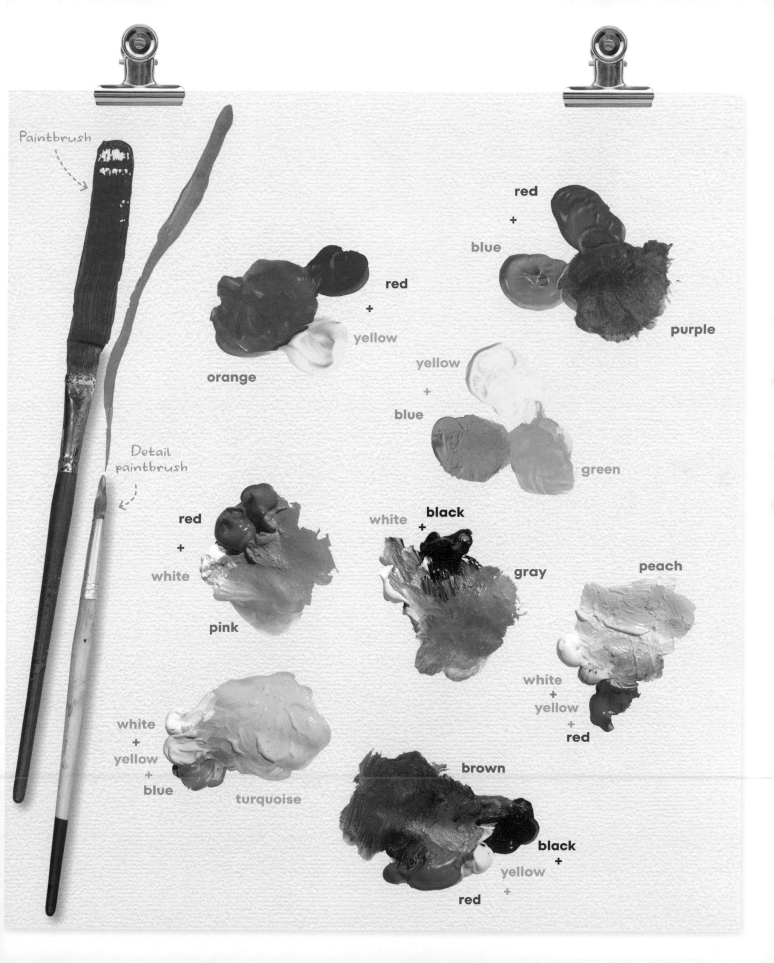

Paintbrush

Detail paintbrush

orange

red
+
yellow

red
+
blue

purple

yellow
+
blue

green

red
+
white

pink

white
black
+

gray

peach

white
+
yellow
+
red

white
+
yellow
+
blue

turquoise

brown

black
+
yellow
+
red

I know how to use glue

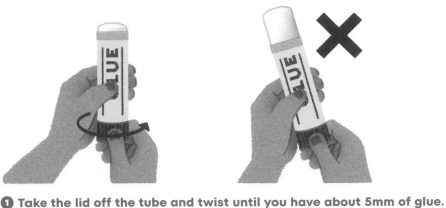

Be quick, because the glue will start to dry!

1 Take the lid off the tube and twist until you have about 5mm of glue.

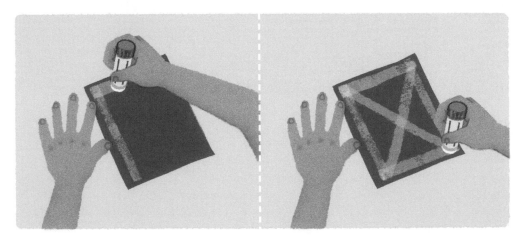

2 Turn the paper over and hold it steady at the edge with one hand. With the other hand, apply the glue around the edges of the paper and a big cross in the center.

3 Turn the paper back again with the tips of your fingers.

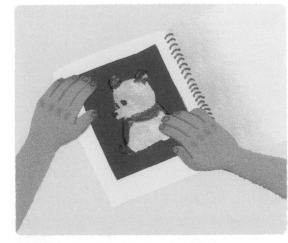

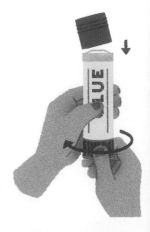

4 Position the paper.

5 Press down all over, especially at the corners.

6 Twist the glue back into the tube, and put the lid back on.

I know how to use tape

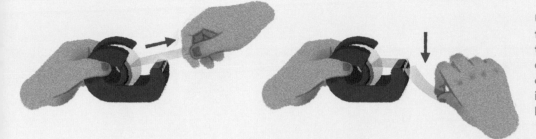

Using your thumb and forefinger, gently pull the tape out and then downward to break off a piece. If you do it too fast, you will have too much tape.

Securing

1 Place the tape half onto the paper and half onto the backing.

2 With one finger, press down to secure it.

Securing with invisible tape

The sticky side on the outside

1 Make a loop with the tape.

2 Put this onto the back of the paper.

3 Turn this over and press down.

Repairing torn paper

1 Put the torn pieces close together.

2 Position the tape over the tear, then press down, avoiding wrinkles.

I know how to wrap a present

Wrapping the present with paper

1 Place the object onto the wrapping paper.

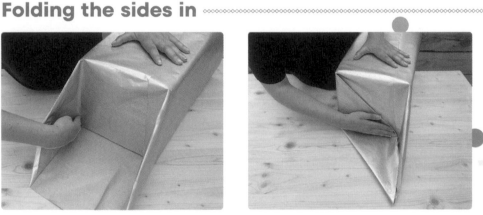

2 Wrap the paper around your object.

3 Carefully cut off the amount of paper needed. Ask your adult if you need help.

Folding the sides in

6 Fold the sides of the paper.

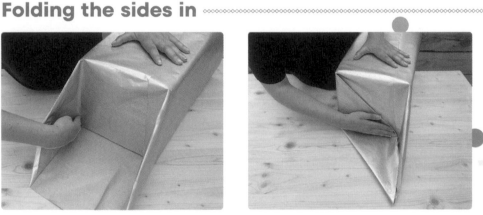

7 Hold the paper against the object.

8 Carefully fold in the paper.

Putting ribbon on

11 Place the present bottom side up onto your length of ribbon.

12 Cross the two ends of ribbon over.

13 Turn the present over.

Cut some small pieces of tape before you begin.

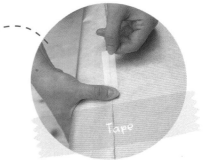

4 Fold the paper snugly around the object to completely cover it.

5 Apply the first piece of tape.

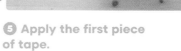

Tape

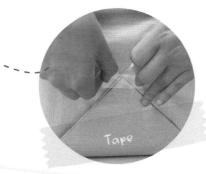

9 To keep the present from opening...

10 ... put on some tape!

Tape

Curl the ribbon

14 Tie the ribbon into a bow.

THANK YOU!

81

I know how to send a letter

Start with the first name then family name.

Stay within this zone.

Sarah West
302 Lorene Avenue
Athens
Ohio OH 45791

The street then the town, followed by the state and the ZIP code.

1 Prepare the envelope. Write the recipient's name and address on the front.

Mia Frost, 42 West Elm Street, Tucson, Arizona AZ 85715

2 Write your address on the back.

Dear Sarah
Thank you for my birthday gift. I have already used it when riding my bike near my grandma's house.
Hope to see you soon!

3 Fold your letter and put it inside the envelope.

Mia Frost, 42 West Elm Street, Tucson, Arizona AZ 85715

4 Either peel the protective paper off the adhesive band, or lick the line of glue on the envelope, fold it down, and press to seal the envelope.

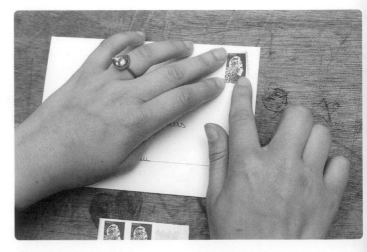

5 Stick your stamp in the top right-hand corner.

Then put it in the mailbox

Sarah West
302 Lorene Avenue
Athens
Ohio OH 45791

I know how to tell the time

①

First of all, look at the short hand—this shows the hours.

The short hand turns slowly, and it takes 12 hours to go all the way around.

②

Now look at the big hand— this shows the minutes.

The big hand turns more quickly, and it takes one hour to go all the way around.

What time is it?

It is 8 o'clock

+

45 minutes

=

It is 8:45 am
or 8:45 pm

It is 4 o'clock

+

10 minutes

=

It is 4:10 am
or 4:10 pm

It is between 2
and 3 o'clock

+

57 minutes

=

It is 2:57 am
or 2:57 pm

84

TICK TOCK

This is the noise of the seconds.

Practise!

With two matchsticks for the hands:

A big one for the minutes...

... and a small one for the hours.

WE CAN ALSO SAY

11:15 or quarter past eleven

11:40 or twenty to twelve

11:45 or quarter to twelve

12:00	12:15	12:30	12:45	13:00
It is midday.	It is quarter past twelve.	It is half past twelve.	It is quarter to one.	It is 1 pm.

85

In the kitchen

I know how to

I know how to set the table

❶ PREPARING THE DISHES AND CUTLERY:
One set of cutlery per person.

❷ Place forks to the left of the plate and knives to the right.

Put the cutlery onto the stacked plates. Carry them carefully to the table with both hands.

❸ The small spoon is always placed between the plate and the glass pointing in the same direction.

❹ A chair can be placed in front of every plate.

❺ YOU CAN ALSO BRING...

If the glasses are stacked into each other, always hold them with one hand under and one hand over.

TIME TO EAT!

I know how to serve myself

Soup

Fill up the ladle with soup, wait until it has stopped dripping, and then pour into your bowl.

Salad

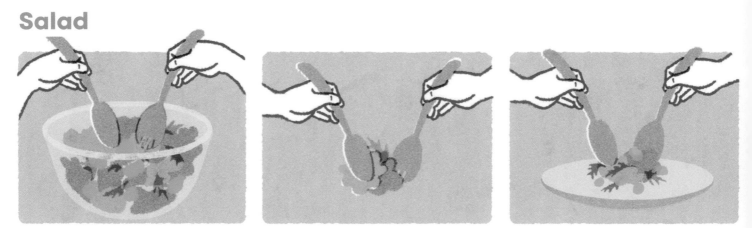

Using the salad spoons, take hold of some salad. Keep the spoons gently squeezed together until you reach your plate.

Spaghetti

Use the spaghetti spoon with the teeth downward, dip into the spaghetti, and then turn it over onto your plate.

90

Water

Hold the base of the carafe with one hand...

... and support the neck of the carafe with the other hand.

Never touch pots and pans that are hot, and take care around hot food in case it splashes.

I know how to use cutlery

Spearing

Scooping

Cutting

Pushing

CHOPSTICKS

① How to hold:
Position the first chopstick between your thumb and third finger. Position the second chopstick between your thumb, forefinger, and middle finger.

② How to open them:
The chopstick on the bottom does not move—it's the top chopstick that opens and closes (a little bit like a crocodile).

Ta-da!

93

I know how to slice bread

WARNING!
This activity can be dangerous and lead to injury. Ask your adult if you need help.

1 Wash your hands before touching food.

2 Place your hand on the bread to hold it steady on the board. Keep your fingers away from the blade to avoid cutting yourself.

3 Using your other hand, hold the bread knife by the handle. Place your forefinger on top and the teeth at the bottom.

4 Slowly and carefully push the knife forward and backward while also pressing onto the knife until you have cut a slice of bread.

BAGUETTE

1 Cut a piece to the necessary size.

2 Place your hand flat on the bread with your fingers nicely aligned. Turn the knife onto its side to cut the baguette in half longways. Do this slowly and carefully, and watch out for your fingers.

Done!

95

I know how to prepare peas and green beans

You'll need...

the vegetables

a colander to put the vegetables into

a bowl for the peelings

Shelling peas

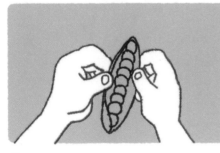

1 Open the peapod with your thumbs.

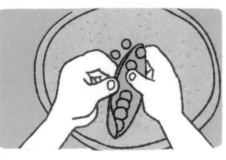

2 Using your thumb, push the peas along the inside of the pod, and let them fall into a colander.

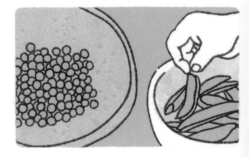

3 The empty pods can be left in the bowl.

Trim the beans

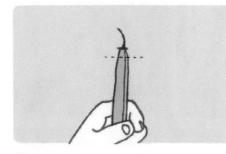

1 Break off the tip of the green bean using your thumb and forefinger.

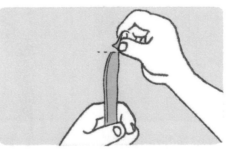

2 Do the same thing to the other end of the bean.

3 Throw the peelings into a bowl.

I know how to wash lettuce

1 Choose a head of lettuce.

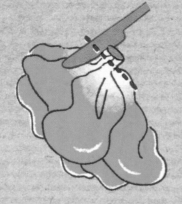
2 Cut off the root part.

3 Gently pull off the leaves.

4 Put the leaves into cold water.

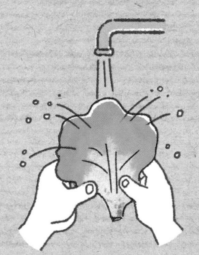
5 Clean them by rubbing your thumbs over them, then rinse under fresh water.

Now add your favorite seasoning!

6 Put the leaves into a salad spinner.

7 Keep turning until they are well drained.

97

I know how to use a peeler

Take hold of the vegetable you are going to peel

Potatoes, beets, turnips, or sweet potatoes...

... carrots, parsnips, or radishes...

... cucumbers, zucchini, or eggplants...

Slide the peeler along the skin

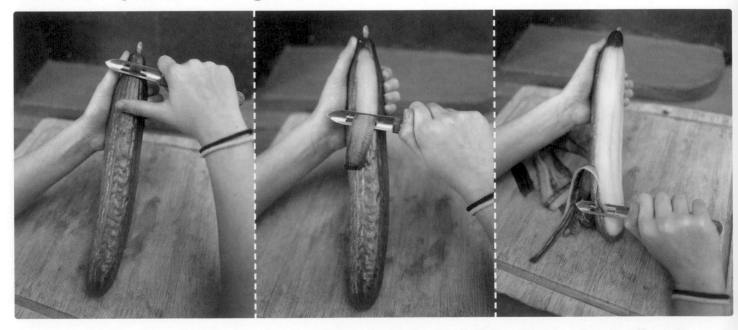

Press the blade into the end of the skin of the vegetable. Carefully slide it all the way down to take off a strip.
Be sure to keep your fingers out of the way of the blade.

I know how to chop vegetables

Into cubes

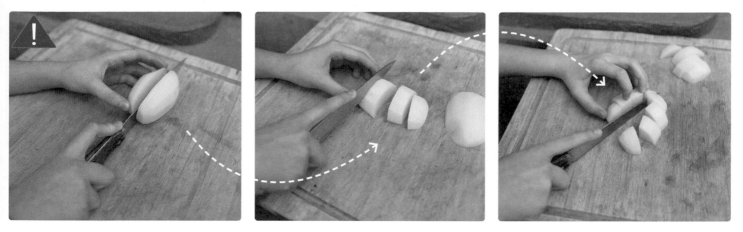

Into slices

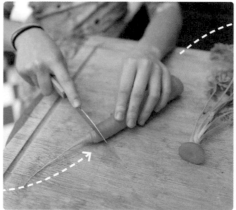

Into sticks

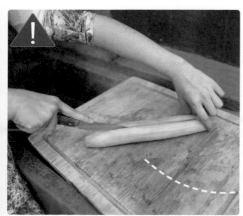

I know how to peel fruit

We eat them with the skin on	We eat them without their skin
blackberries	pineapple
strawberries	banana
plums	orange
redcurrants	kiwi
tomatoes	lychee

BANANA

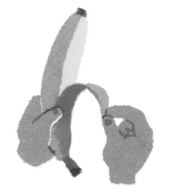

1 Detach one banana from the bunch.

2 Hold the banana with the stalk at the bottom.

3 From the top, pull down strips of the skin.

Yum!

kiwi
★ ★ ★

1 Using a knife, cut the kiwi in half. Remember to keep your fingers out of the way.

2 Scoop your kiwi out with a spoon...

3 ... until there is only the skin left.

clementine

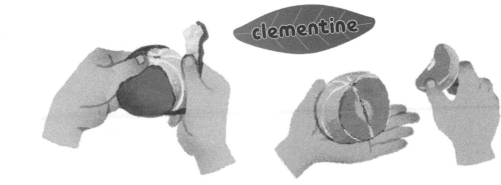

1 Dig your fingernail into the skin to make a small hole.

2 Slide your finger under the skin and push to remove it.

3 You can enjoy eating the segments one at a time.

101

I know how to remove the pit

1 With a knife, cut off a slice.

2 Continue all the way around the fruit until there is only the pit left.

3 Pull the pit away with your fingers.

 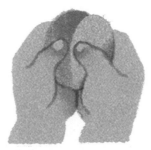 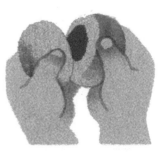

1 Place your thumbs on each side of the groove and pull apart.

2 Pull the pit away with your fingers.

You can put the whole cherry into your mouth, then carefully spit out the pit.

Always wash fruit...

... before eating the skin!

I know how to crack open nuts

CRACK!

❶ Hold the nutcracker in your hand. Put the nut into it with the other hand.

❷ Tighten the nutcracker around the nut until it cracks. Be sure to keep your fingers out of the way.

❸ Remove the broken shell from the kernel.

For smaller nuts— like hazelnuts— place them higher up in the nutcracker.

103

I know how to prepare an apple

How to cut

Using a thin-bladed knife, cut the apple in half from top to bottom. Then, cut these two halves in half again so you have quarters. Do this slowly and carefully, and keep your fingers away from the blade!

Removing the seeds

Just above the seeds, cut into the apple. Turn the apple around and do the same on the other side.

You can even just bite into the apple without peeling it!

How to peel

Holding one of the quarters in your hand and the knife in the other, start at one end and peel away the skin as thinly as possible. Watch those fingers!

I know how to make chocolate

~~~~~~~~~~ **CHOCOLATE MILK** ~~~~~~~~~~

1 Fill up your mug with either cow's milk or plant-based milk, such as rice milk or oat milk.

2 Add two teaspoons of cocoa powder.

3 Mix well.

milk and a sandwich

SANDWICH

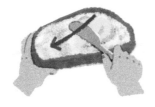

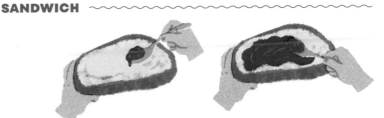

❶ Take a small amount of butter.

❷ Keeping the knife flat, spread this evenly onto your bread.

❸ Using the back of a teaspoon, spread your jam or honey onto the bread.

107

I know how to crack an egg

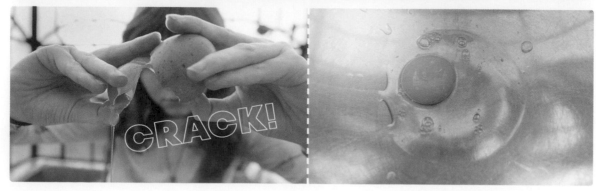

1
Take an egg and gently tap it onto the side of the bowl.

2
Place the tips of your thumbs on either side of the crack with your fingernails in the crack.

3
Holding the egg above the bowl, press lightly with your thumbs and gently pull the egg shell apart.

I know how to make an omelet

WARNING!
This activity can be dangerous and lead to injury. Pots and pans get VERY hot and can cause serious burns. Ask your adult if you need help.

❶ Crack your eggs.

❷ Beat the eggs with a whisk.

❸ Add a pinch of salt for seasoning.

❹ Carefully pour the eggs into a hot, oiled frying pan. Beware—the pan may spatter.

❺ With a spatula, loosen the edges around your omelet. Pan handles can get hot, so make sure to protect your hands.

❻ Fold your omelet over.

❼ Slide it onto a plate.

A REAL CHEF!

I know how to boil an egg

Cooking technique

1 Bring a pan of water to a boil. Take care—boiling water burns.

2 Using a spoon, carefully place the eggs in the water and set the timer.

3 When the time is up, remove the pan from the heat using both hands.

3 minute soft-boiled egg

1 Using a large spoon, place your eggs into the egg cups.

2 Once the egg has cooled down a little bit, open it using the edge of the spoon.

3 Your soft-boiled egg will be delicious with buttered bread and some cheese.

10 minute hard-boiled egg

1 Immediately put the cooked eggs into a bowl of cold water.

2 Once the eggs have cooled a little, break the shell.

3 Peel the shell away from the egg with your fingers.

4 Rinse your eggs.

5 Carefully cut them in half.

Try...
- with mayonnaise
- with a little salt
- in a salad
- in your lunch box

I know how to cook pasta

① Fill a pan with water and a pinch of salt, then put it on the heat.

② Put the lid on the pan.

③ As soon as the water starts to boil, remove the lid.

④ Pour the pasta into the water and stir with a wooden spoon.

⑤ Set the timer for the cooking time shown on the packet of pasta.

Use a large pan for spaghetti to avoid having to break the noodles.

⑥ Put a colander into the sink and carefully pour the pasta into it.

⑦ Add your favorite seasoning.

Boiling water can cause serious burns. Follow the steps slowly and carefully.

Pasta comes in many
shapes with many
different names:
Conchiglie
Tagliatelle
Ravioli
Penne
Farfalle
Rigatoni
Linguine
Radiatori
Macaroni
Tortellini

I know how to bake a cake

PREPARE THE INGREDIENTS

yogurt

sugar

eggs

baking powder

flour

salt

oil

YOGURT CAKE
USE THE EMPTY YOGURT POT TO MEASURE OUT THE REST OF THE INGREDIENTS.
Serves 4
1 pot of yogurt
2 pots of granulated sugar
1 pot of oil
3 pots of flour
3 eggs
1 pinch of salt
1 teaspoon of baking powder

❶

Preheat the oven to 350°F.

❷

Mix together in the following order: the yogurt, the sugar, the oil, the flour, the baking powder, the eggs, and then the salt.

❸

Pour the mixture into a greased and floured cake pan or a bread pan.

❹

Cook in the oven for about 40 minutes.

❺

Allow it to cool before removing the cake from the pan.

PREPARE THE BOWLS AND UTENSILS

1 wooden spoon

1 mixing bowl

1 bread pan
OR

1 cake pan

To add your personal touch to the cake, you can:

Use ground hazelnuts instead of flour

Add some red fruit jam

Use a fruit yogurt

Add dried fruit or chocolate chips

① Preheat the oven

Set the temperature of the oven as soon as you get into the kitchen.

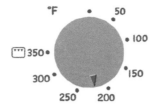

°F
50
100
350
150
300
250   200

② Mixing the ingredients

yogurt

oil

flour and baking powder

sugar

eggs

pinch of salt

Mix together using a wooden spoon. Squash the lumps with the back of the spoon, and mix until the batter is smooth.

115

❸ Prepare the cake pan and pour in the batter

Rub the inside of the pan with a small square of butter...

... or instead, you could use parchment paper.

Pour the batter into the pan, scraping around the bowl with the spoon.

❹ Place it in the oven and supervise the cooking

The oven will be hot now, so be careful not to burn yourself.

Poke the tip of a knife into the cake. Wet = the cake is not cooked yet. Dry = the cake is ready!

Take your cake out of the oven using oven mitts, and put it onto a heatproof surface.

❺ Allow your cake to cool down before removing it from the pan!

Slide the tip of a knife around the edge of your cake.

Turn it over onto a plate.

Serve yourself a slice and enjoy!

117

I know how to put away groceries

If you're not sure where your shopping needs to go, think about where you found it in the supermarket.

1 All the products that must be kept cold can be put into the fridge.

Try not to leave the door open for too long so it stays cold in there!

Sorbet

Petits Pois

PIZZA

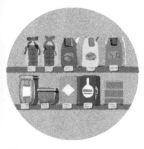

2 The products that do not need to be kept cold can be put away in the cabinets or pantry.

As long as they have never been opened, some bottles of milk or juice can be stored out of the fridge. You'll find this information written on the label.

Put flowers and fresh herbs in a little water.

3 All beauty and personal hygiene products can be kept in the bathroom cabinets.

SOAP

4 Always store the cleaning products out of reach of children.

POWER · CLEAN

119

At home

I know how to

I know how to reduce waste

At the  supermarket

Choose loose items and refillable products.

Only buy what you need.

Always take your own bag.

Return items that can be reused.

At home

Don't waste anything.

Don't use single-use products.

Keep the leftovers.

Give away rather than throw away.

Reuse things for another purpose.

Repair rather than buy new.

Sort the waste, as some things can be recycled.

I know how to sort out the recycling

Empty cans, bottles, packets, and paper

Flatten cardboard boxes

Glass

Bottle tops and corks

Compost

Broken glass

Find out from the local government what the guidelines are for organizing your waste. Sometimes these are different depending on where you live.

Everything else!

If you don't know where to throw waste, put it in the trash bin!

I know how to clean up with a sponge

Preparing the sponge

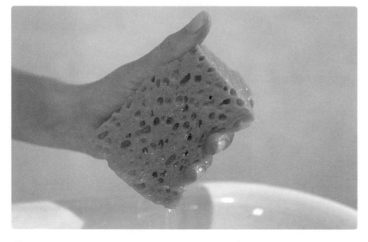

1 Wet the sponge under the tap or in a bowl of clean water.

2 Squeeze it well so that it is not dripping.

If you have spilled food

Press the side of the sponge onto the table to collect the spill, then turn it toward you.

If you have spilled a liquid

Repeat until all the liquid has been absorbed.

Put the sponge onto the liquid to absorb it, then squeeze it out into the sink.

Cleaning a table

Always rinse and squeeze the sponge both between cleaning and when you have finished.

① With the sponge, gather all of the crumbs toward the edge of the table.

② Push the crumbs either into your hand or onto a plate.

③ Dry the table off with a kitchen towel.

125

I know how to fill the dishwasher

Only start the dishwasher once it is completely full!

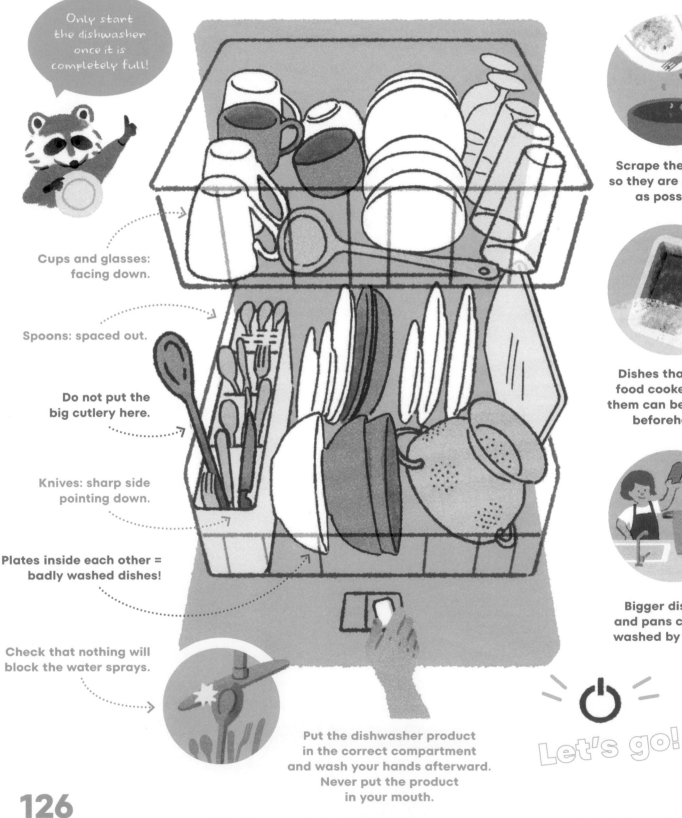

Cups and glasses: facing down.

Spoons: spaced out.

Do not put the big cutlery here.

Knives: sharp side pointing down.

Plates inside each other = badly washed dishes!

Check that nothing will block the water sprays.

Put the dishwasher product in the correct compartment and wash your hands afterward. Never put the product in your mouth.

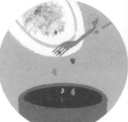

Scrape the dishes so they are as clean as possible.

Dishes that have food cooked onto them can be soaked beforehand.

Bigger dishes and pans can be washed by hand.

Let's go!

I know how to wash the dishes

MY PLATE OR BOWL

1 Put a dot of dishwashing liquid onto the sponge.

2 Use the scratchy side for difficult stains.

3 Don't forget the edges or the outside.

4 Rinse the whole thing under warm water.

If the plates are very greasy, you can wipe them over with some kitchen paper before washing.

LOTS OF DISHES

1 Fill the sink with warm water and a little dishwashing liquid.

2 Wash following the order of not too dirty to very dirty: glasses, cutlery, plates, then the bigger dishes.

3 For the dishes with food stuck onto them, you can let them soak.

4 Allow the dishes, glasses, and cutlery to drain, then dry them with a clean, dry kitchen towel.

5 You can stack the plates, bowls, and glasses before you put them away.

I know how to clean the floor

1 Using a broom, sweep dirt into a small pile.

2 Place the dustpan next to the pile of dirt.

3 Carefully sweep the dirt onto the dustpan and tip into the trash.

 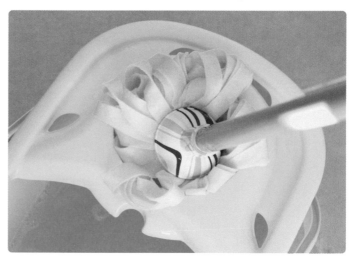

4 Fill a bucket with warm, soapy water.

5 Dip a clean mop into the bucket. Then, push it into the squeezer, and twist it until it stops dripping.

 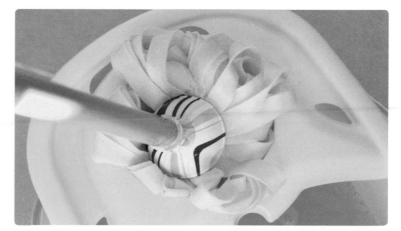

6 Wipe the mop backward and forward across the floor. Start as far away from the door as you can so that you can still get out when the floor is wet.

7 When the mop gets dirty or begins to dry out, repeat step 5. Then carry on mopping.

129

I know how to wash and hang

Whites

Colors

Darks

Wool

1 Sort the washing by color—whites, bright colors, darks—and turn jeans inside out.

Any delicate washing, like silk or wool, can be left to one side to be put on the "delicate" cycle.

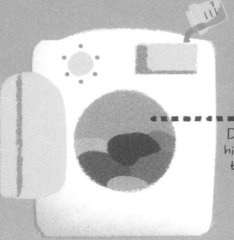

Do not fill higher than this level!

2 Fill the machine, but not too full!

3 Add the detergent powder, liquid, or pod. The label will tell you how much. You should never put these in your mouth.

4 Choose the right cycle on the washing machine. Ask your adult if you're not sure which one to use.

Getting rid of a stain

1 Dampen the stained area.

2 Add a little soap.

3 Rub it and rinse with water.

out clothes

5 When the cycle has finished, take the washing out, and put it into a basket so you can take it to be hung out.

6 Before you hang it up, firmly shake out the wrinkles and the folds.

Pinch together to open.

7 Hang t-shirts from the bottom, pegging from the seams.

8 Hang pants from the waist.

9 Lie sweaters and cardigans flat to keep them from losing their shape.

Do not put the clothes too close together—allow the air to circulate.

Do not put wet clothes to dry on a radiator.

I know how to sew a button

Preparing the needle ◇◇

❶ Cut off a length of thread about as long as your arm. Insert the thread through the eye of the needle and pull it through a little.

Sewing the button ◇◇

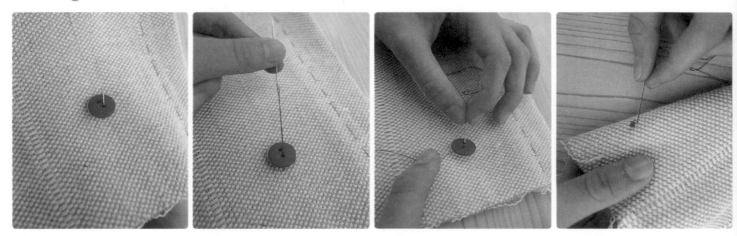

❸ Sew two stitches on the back of the garment. From behind, push the needle through one of the little holes on the button, then back through the other. Pull this through at the back. The needle will be sharp, so be careful.

Repeat steps ❸ to ❺ several times.

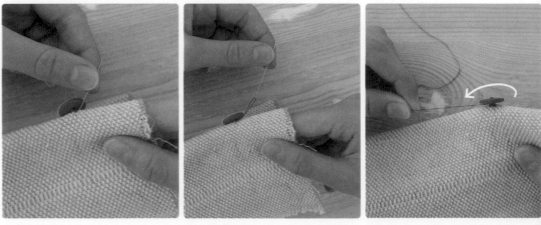

❻ Insert the needle between the button and the garment. Wind the thread around and under the button.

132

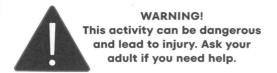
❷ Tie a knot at the end of the long thread.

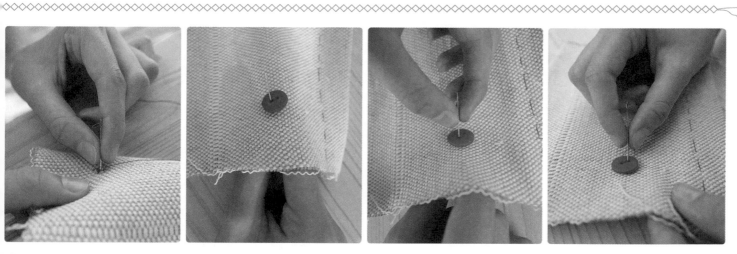

❹ Insert the needle from behind through the other little hole, and pull it through with the other hand.

❺ Put it back through the opposite little hole.

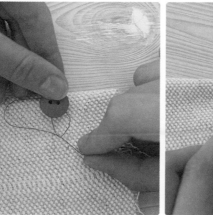

❼ Tie a knot and then cut the thread.

Fixed!

I know how to take care of a pet

My cat

- Brush your cat regularly and always in the direction of hair growth.
- You can use a scoop and a bag to clean up the litter every day.
- Clean out the litter box once a week.

My rabbit

- Remove the rabbit's droppings with a small scoop.
- Make sure there is always fresh water every day.

My goldfish

- Feed your fish with one or two pinches of flakes every day.
- When you change the water each week, you can put your fish into another bowl of water.

My dog

- Your dog needs to be walked several times a day.
- You will need a leash and some small waste bags to pick up the poop.

I know how to be careful

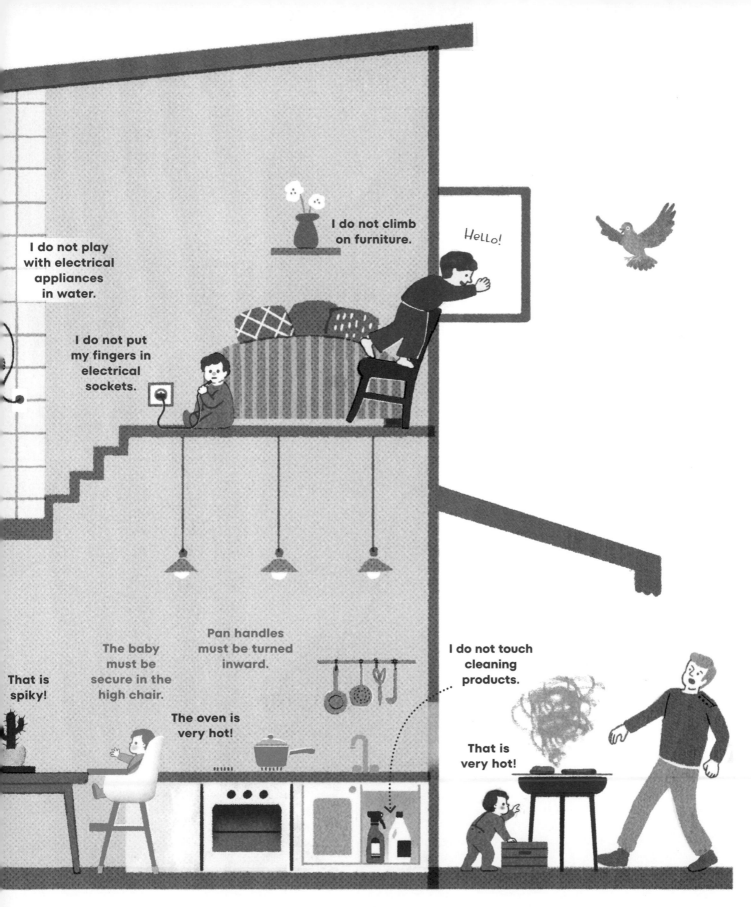

Outdoors

I know how to

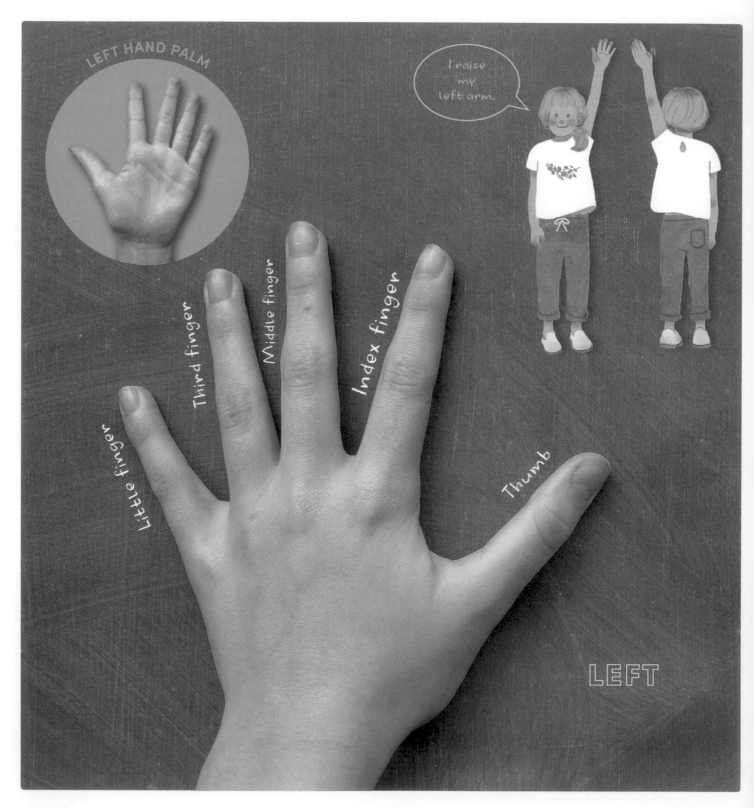

my right

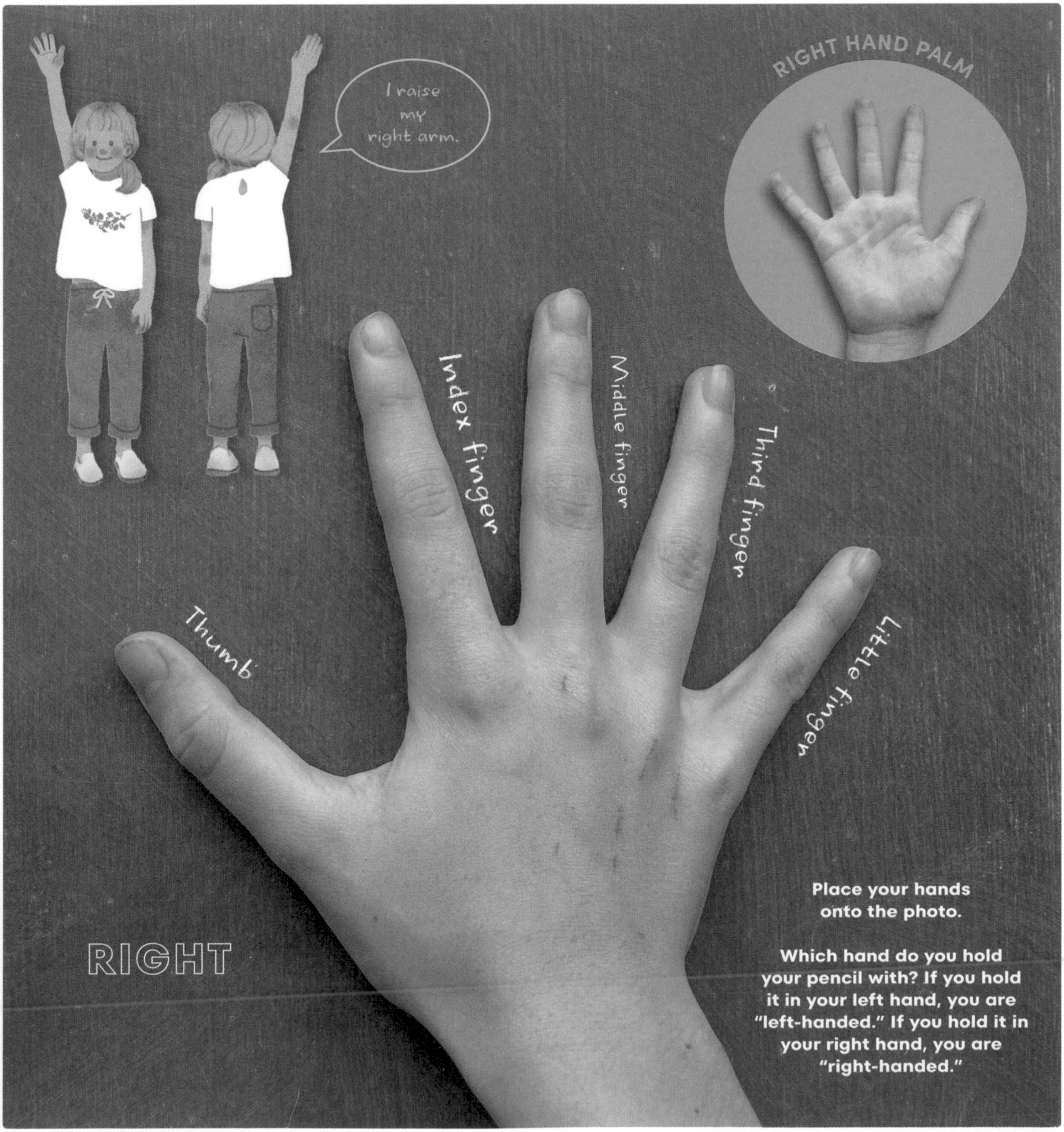

I raise my right arm.

RIGHT HAND PALM

Index finger

Middle finger

Third finger

Little finger

Thumb

RIGHT

Place your hands onto the photo.

Which hand do you hold your pencil with? If you hold it in your left hand, you are "left-handed." If you hold it in your right hand, you are "right-handed."

I know how to cross the road

I stand at the crossing and wait until the cars stop, or for the walking figure to light up.

I look to the left and then right, and keep looking both ways while I cross.

Don't ever cross behind a truck or a bus. You cannot see vehicles coming from the other direction, and they can't see you either!

WHEN THERE ARE NO TRAFFIC LIGHTS OR A CROSSWALK:

Choose a place where you can see the cars coming from far away and they can see you. Looking from left to right, cross when there are no cars or if they have stopped.

I know how to get around safely

Spot the mistakes in this picture!

looking at the phone while crossing ○ wearing headphones while riding a bike ○ running while crossing the road ○ two people on one bike ○ riding a bike without a helmet ○ playing with a ball in the street ○ crossing in front of a parking lot or garage without looking ○ walking in the gutter ○ putting a hand outside of the car window ○ riding a bike with no hands

I know how to follow directions

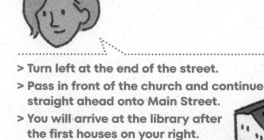

Could you tell me how to get to the library, please?

> Turn left at the end of the street.
> Pass in front of the church and continue straight ahead onto Main Street.
> You will arrive at the library after the first houses on your right.

CHURCH

MAIN

ST.

CHURCH STREET

BREAD STREET

LITTLE WOOD ROAD

BOULEVARD

HALF

MOON STREET

PASTURE

PHARMACY

MECHANIC

CENTRAL AVENUE

SCHOOL

NEWTON

GYM

ROAD

QUAY

BRYANT

BOULEVARD

NORTH

I can't remember how to get to the carousel.

> Take the first right after the gym.
> Go straight toward the river and cross over the bridge.
> Continue straight in front of the town hall until you get to the square where the carousel is.

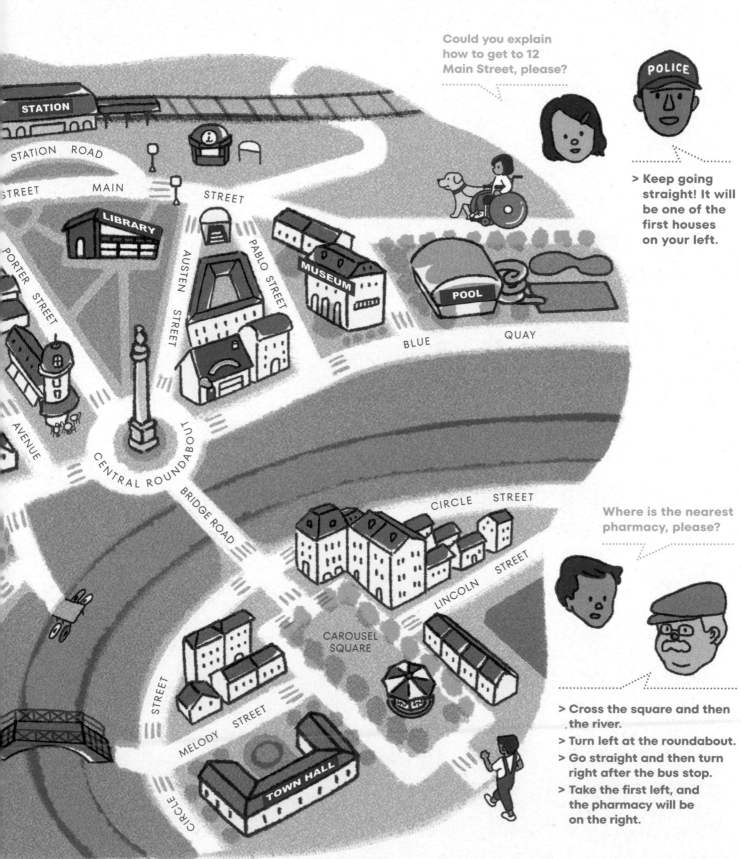

Could you explain how to get to 12 Main Street, please?

> Keep going straight! It will be one of the first houses on your left.

Where is the nearest pharmacy, please?

> Cross the square and then the river.
> Turn left at the roundabout.
> Go straight and then turn right after the bus stop.
> Take the first left, and the pharmacy will be on the right.

I know how to buy bread

I know how to fasten my seatbelt

1 Slowly pull the seatbelt—it will lock itself if you pull too quickly.

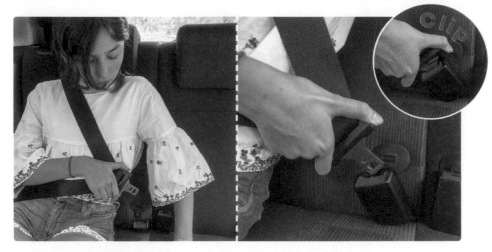

2 Push the metal end piece into the clip.

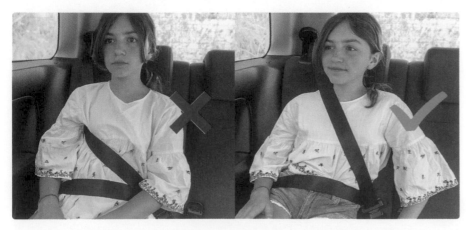

The strap must be positioned over your shoulder, not under your arm.

If you are smaller than 4ft, 9in in height, you must use a booster seat.

UNFASTENING THE SEATBELT:
Press the red button and pull the clip toward you.

BEFORE OPENING THE DOOR:
Always make sure that there are no vehicles or pedestrians.

I know how to take the bus

I know how to swim

Breaststroke

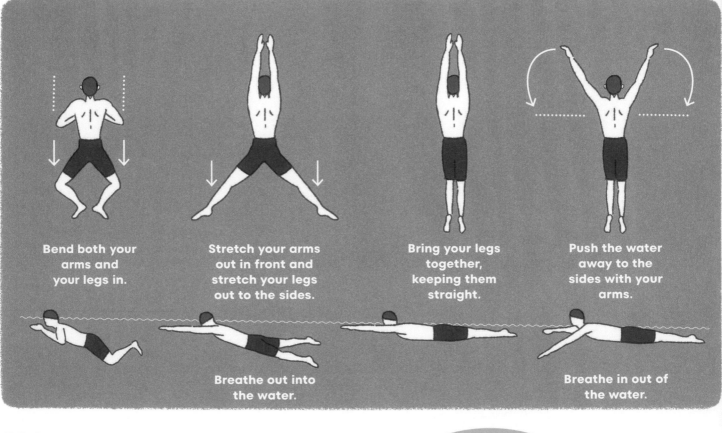

Bend both your arms and your legs in.

Stretch your arms out in front and stretch your legs out to the sides.

Bring your legs together, keeping them straight.

Push the water away to the sides with your arms.

Breathe out into the water.

Breathe in out of the water.

Diving

Read signs to check whether diving is allowed, and always make sure that the water is deep enough to dive into.

① Feet together with your arms stretched above your head. ② Bend your knees and lean forward. ③ Push with your legs. ④ Bring your head in. ⑤ Straighten out your legs. ⑥ Point your feet.

I know how to ride a bike

Look forward...
the bike will go in
the direction that
you are looking!

Your seat is at a
comfortable height
when the tips of
your toes touch
the ground.

Arms are bent
slightly.

Make sure
your laces are
not too long.

Tire pressure
is good.

① Sit on your bicycle.

② Put one foot onto a pedal and push hard to get your momentum!

③ Now put your other foot onto the other pedal.

You could even begin without pedals, just to find your balance.

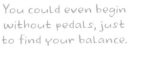

PUTTING ON A HELMET

① Put the helmet on your head, making sure it is straight and comfortable.

② Fasten the clip under your chin.

③ Pull the strap to adjust.

TAKING IT OFF:
Press the two red teeth in and pull.

④ If necessary, you can turn the little knob at the back to tighten.

To lock up my bike, I put the chain through the bike frame and around the bike rack.

④ Push down on the pedals to make the bike move forward.

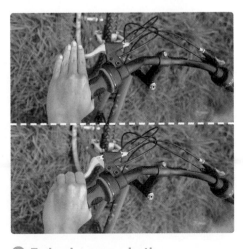

⑤ To brake, press both brakes slowly with the ends of your fingers.

⑥ When you stop, put one foot on the ground with the bike leaning to one side.

At school

I know how to

I know how to say the alphabet

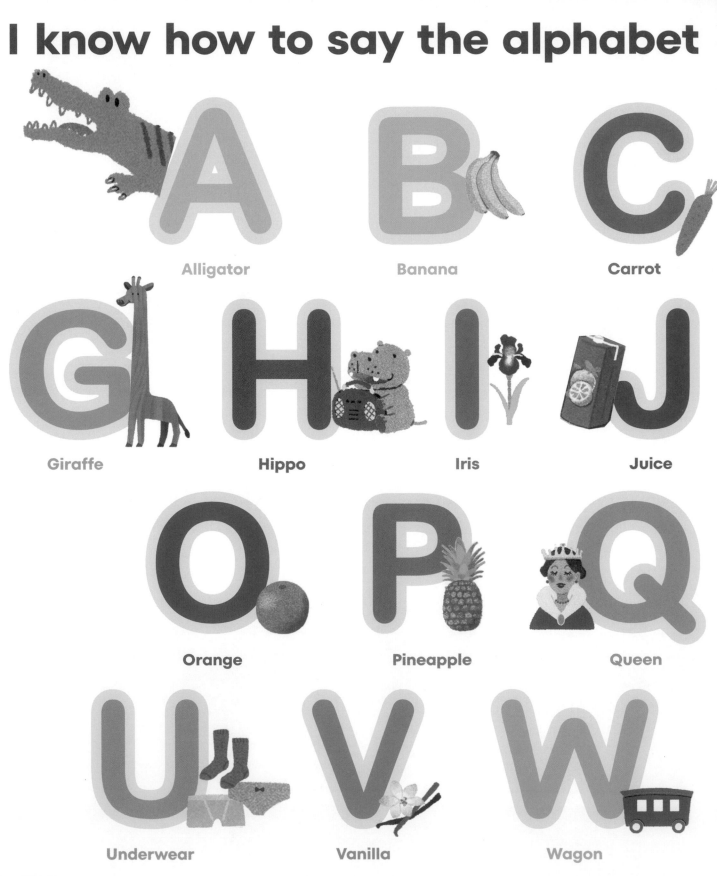

A Alligator

B Banana

C Carrot

G Giraffe

H Hippo

I Iris

J Juice

O Orange

P Pineapple

Q Queen

U Underwear

V Vanilla

W Wagon

D

Dice

E

Egg

F

Factory

K

Kiwi

L

Leek

M

Milk

N

Nuts

R

Radish

S

Snail

T

Tomato

X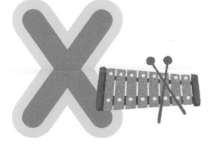

Xylophone

Y

Yogurt

Z

Zebra

159

I know how to count to 100

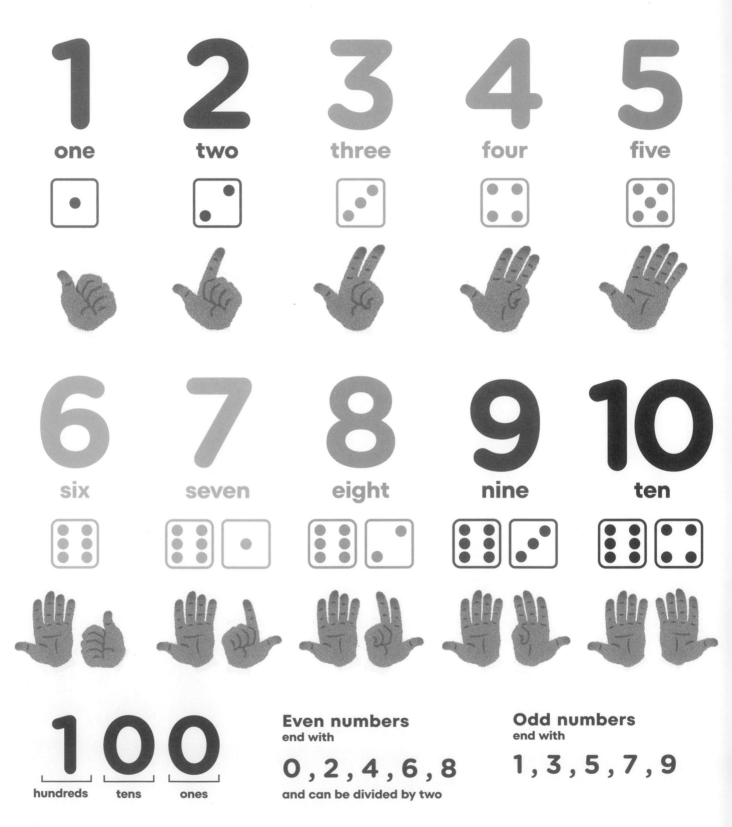

1 one

2 two

3 three

4 four

5 five

6 six

7 seven

8 eight

9 nine

10 ten

100
hundreds tens ones

Even numbers
end with

0 , 2 , 4 , 6 , 8

and can be divided by two

Odd numbers
end with

1 , 3 , 5 , 7 , 9

0 zero	**1** one	**2** two	**3** three	**4** four	**5** five	**6** six	**7** seven	**8** eight	**9** nine
10 ten	**11** eleven	**12** twelve	**13** thirteen	**14** fourteen	**15** fifteen	**16** sixteen	**17** seventeen	**18** eighteen	**19** nineteen
20 twenty	**21** twenty-one	**22** twenty-two	**23** twenty-three	**24** twenty-four	**25** twenty-five	**26** twenty-six	**27** twenty-seven	**28** twenty-eight	**29** twenty-nine
30 thirty	**31** thirty-one	**32** thirty-two	**33** thirty-three	**34** thirty-four	**35** thirty-five	**36** thirty-six	**37** thirty-seven	**38** thirty-eight	**39** thirty-nine
40 forty	**41** forty-one	**42** forty-two	**43** forty-three	**44** forty-four	**45** forty-five	**46** forty-six	**47** forty-seven	**48** forty-eight	**49** forty-nine
50 fifty	**51** fifty-one	**52** fifty-two	**53** fifty-three	**54** fifty-four	**55** fifty-five	**56** fifty-six	**57** fifty-seven	**58** fifty-eight	**59** fifty-nine
60 sixty	**61** sixty-one	**62** sixty-two	**63** sixty-three	**64** sixty-four	**65** sixty-five	**66** sixty-six	**67** sixty-seven	**68** sixty-eight	**69** sixty-nine
70 seventy	**71** seventy-one	**72** seventy-two	**73** seventy-three	**74** seventy-four	**75** seventy-five	**76** seventy-six	**77** seventy-seven	**78** seventy-eight	**79** seventy-nine
80 eighty	**81** eighty-one	**82** eighty-two	**83** eighty-three	**84** eighty-four	**85** eighty-five	**86** eighty-six	**87** eighty-seven	**88** eighty-eight	**89** eighty-nine
90 ninety	**91** ninety-one	**92** ninety-two	**93** ninety-three	**94** ninety-four	**95** ninety-five	**96** ninety-six	**97** ninety-seven	**98** ninety-eight	**99** ninety-nine
100 one hundred	**101** one hundred and one	**102** one hundred and two	**103** one hundred and three	**104** one hundred and four	**105** one hundred and five	**...**			

I know how to do my times tables

1

1 × 1 = 1
2 × 1 = 2
3 × 1 = 3
4 × 1 = 4
5 × 1 = 5
6 × 1 = 6
7 × 1 = 7
8 × 1 = 8
9 × 1 = 9
10 × 1 = 10

2

1 × 2 = 2
2 × 2 = 4
3 × 2 = 6
4 × 2 = 8
5 × 2 = 10
6 × 2 = 12
7 × 2 = 14
8 × 2 = 16
9 × 2 = 18
10 × 2 = 20

3

1 × 3 = 3
2 × 3 = 6
3 × 3 = 9
4 × 3 = 12
5 × 3 = 15
6 × 3 = 18
7 × 3 = 21
8 × 3 = 24
9 × 3 = 27
10 × 3 = 30

4

1 × 4 = 4
2 × 4 = 8
3 × 4 = 12
4 × 4 = 16
5 × 4 = 20
6 × 4 = 24
7 × 4 = 28
8 × 4 = 32
9 × 4 = 36
10 × 4 = 40

6

1 × 6 = 6
2 × 6 = 12
3 × 6 = 18
4 × 6 = 24
5 × 6 = 30
6 × 6 = 36
7 × 6 = 42
8 × 6 = 48
9 × 6 = 54
10 × 6 = 60

7

1 × 7 = 7
2 × 7 = 14
3 × 7 = 21
4 × 7 = 28
5 × 7 = 35
6 × 7 = 42
7 × 7 = 49
8 × 7 = 56
9 × 7 = 63
10 × 7 = 70

8

1 × 8 = 8
2 × 8 = 16
3 × 8 = 24
4 × 8 = 32
5 × 8 = 40
6 × 8 = 48
7 × 8 = 56
8 × 8 = 64
9 × 8 = 72
10 × 8 = 80

9

1 × 9 = 9
2 × 9 = 18
3 × 9 = 27
4 × 9 = 36
5 × 9 = 45
6 × 9 = 54
7 × 9 = 63
8 × 9 = 72
9 × 9 = 81
10 × 9 = 90

5

1	×	5	=	5
2	×	5	=	10
3	×	5	=	15
4	×	5	=	20
5	×	5	=	25
6	×	5	=	30
7	×	5	=	35
8	×	5	=	40
9	×	5	=	45
10	×	5	=	50

10

1	×	10	=	10
2	×	10	=	20
3	×	10	=	30
4	×	10	=	40
5	×	10	=	50
6	×	10	=	60
7	×	10	=	70
8	×	10	=	80
9	×	10	=	90
10	×	10	=	100

AMAZING TIP FOR THE 9 TIMES TABLE

① Open your hands toward you. Going from the left, fold down the finger that corresponds with the multiple of 9.

② The fingers on the left of the folded-down finger can be considered as the tens...

③ ... and the fingers to the right can be considered as the ones.

$3 \times 9 = 27$

$1 \times 9 = 9$

$5 \times 9 = 45$

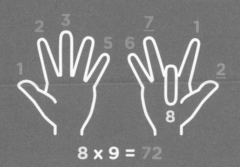

$8 \times 9 = 72$

$10 \times 9 = 90$

I know how to use homophones

HOMOPHONES

What are homophones?

Homophones are words that sound the same but are spelled differently and have different meanings.

Examples of homophones:

reek—The reek of eggs is strong.
wreak—The puppy will wreak havoc in the house.

IT'S AND ITS

It's is a contraction of **it is** or **it has**.

Its means **belonging to it**.

Examples of it's:

It's time for dinner.
I'll call you when **it's** ready.
It's raining tomorrow.

YOU'RE AND YOUR

You're is a contraction of **you are**.

Your means **belonging to you**.

Examples of you're:

You're my older brother.
If **you're** cold, put on a sweater.
You're always late!

THERE, THEIR, AND THEY'RE

Use **there** when referring to a **place**.

Use **their** when something belongs to **them**.

They're is a contraction of **they are**.

All of these words and spellings are correct, but they have different meanings and uses.

Examples of there:

The coat hooks are over **there**.

I've never been to Paris. I would like to go **there**.

I found my socks in **there**.

There is better than here.

Is **there** somewhere I can buy a candy bar?

herd—I saw a herd of cattle.
heard—I heard them talk.
guessed—I guessed his age.
guest—She was a guest.

Chose the correct word in these sentences:

Give it a try

I **herd/heard** a noise.
We have a **guessed/guest** staying with us.
Those shoes **reek/wreak**!
I never would have **guessed/guest** that.

Examples of its:

The clown paints **its** face.
The flag is on **its** pole.
The book fell off **its** shelf.

Chose the correct word in these sentences:

Its/It's not my fault.
The book is on **its/it's** shelf.
Its/It's on **its/it's** way.
When **its/it's** hot, I wear sandals.

Examples of your:

Your teacher is Mr. Smith.
Where is **your** bike?
If **your** pencil breaks, you can borrow mine.

Chose the correct word in these sentences:

How is **your/you're** mom?
Your/you're still at school.
I can call you when **your/you're** at home.
That is **your/you're** favorite coat.

Examples of their:

Their bedroom is bigger than mine.

When I go to **their** house, we make pasta.

Sarah and Amelia decided to share **their** dolls.

They are twins, and **their** faces are identical.

Their dog's name is Spot.

Examples of they're:

They're going to watch a movie.

They said **they're** almost here.

They're never at home.

I'll make the salad when **they're** ready to eat.

When **they're** riding their bikes, time flies.

Chose the correct word in these sentences:

There/their/they're going to be late.

There/their/they're t-shirt has a hole in it.

The book is under **there/their/they're**.

Where are **there/their/they're** pets?

I know how to read a world map

CONTINENTS

- Europe
- North and South America
- Africa
- Asia
- Australasia and Oceania
- Antarctica

PARALLELS OF LATITUDE

These imaginary lines running east to west are parallel to the equator and are used to describe the specific location of a point found north or south of the Equator. This is the latitude of a point.

EQUATOR

An imaginary line running east to west, halfway between the two poles. It represents the division between the northern hemisphere and the southern hemisphere.

MERIDIANS OF LONGITUDE

These are imaginary lines running between the North Pole and the South Pole. This is used to describe the longitude of a point.

The Greenwich Meridian, or Prime Meridian, is the north-south line that measures 0° longitude. This is the international reference for longitude.

midday   midnight

TIME ZONES

These are the zones where time is always the same. Even though they are represented by the longitude lines, they tend to follow different countries' borders.

TIME DIFFERENCE

When it is nighttime in Europe, it is morning in the United States of America.

NORTH
AMERICA

ATLANTIC
OCEAN

Tropic of Cancer

Equator

PACIFIC OCEAN

SOUTH
AMERICA

Tropic of Capricorn

NORTH POLE

ARCTIC OCEAN

EUROPE

ASIA

NORTHERN HEMISPHIRE

AFRICA

PACIFIC OCEAN

INDIAN OCEAN

ATLANTIC OCEAN

AUSTRALASIA AND OCEANIA

Greenwich

ANTARCTIC OCEAN

SOUTHERN HEMISPHERE

ANTARCTICA

SOUTH POLE

I know how to read a map of

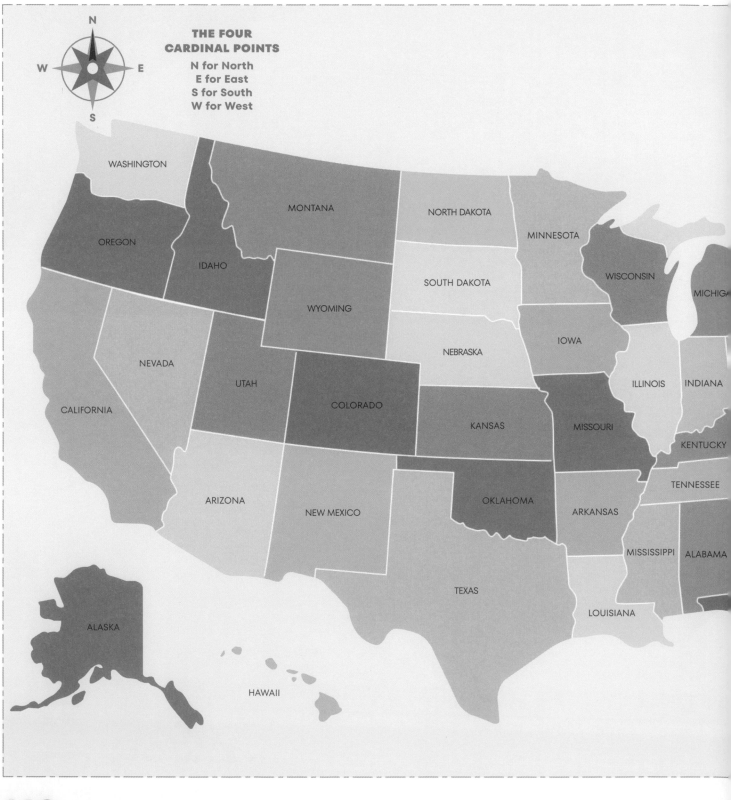

the United States

NEW HAMPSHIRE
MASSACHUSETTS
VERMONT
MAINE
NEW YORK
RHODE ISLAND
PENNSYLVANIA
CONNECTICUT
OHIO
NEW JERSEY
DELAWARE
MARYLAND
WEST VIRGINIA
VIRGINIA
NORTH CAROLINA
SOUTH CAROLINA
GEORGIA
FLORIDA

AMERICAN STATE FLAGS

ALABAMA	ALASKA	ARIZONA	ARKANSAS	CALIFORNIA	COLORADO
CONNECTICUT	DELAWARE	FLORIDA	GEORGIA	HAWAII	IDAHO
ILLINOIS	INDIANA	IOWA	KANSAS	KENTUCKY	LOUISIANA
MAINE	MARYLAND	MASSACHUSETTS	MICHIGAN	MINNESOTA	MISSISSIPPI
MISSOURI	MONTANA	NEBRASKA	NEVADA	NEW HAMPSHIRE	NEW JERSEY
NEW MEXICO	NEW YORK	NORTH CAROLINA	NORTH DAKOTA	OHIO	OKLAHOMA
OREGON	PENNSYLVANIA	RHODE ISLAND	SOUTH CAROLINA	SOUTH DAKOTA	TENNESSEE
TEXAS	UTAH	VERMONT	VIRGINIA	WASHINGTON	WEST VIRGINIA
WISCONSIN	WYOMING				

I know how to understand my rights

The United Nations Convention on the Rights of a Child (UNCRC) is an international agreement that recognizes and protects children's rights.

The right to have a name, a nationality, and an identity.

The right to be taken care of, to be protected from illness, and to have access to a balanced and healthy diet.

The right to not take part in war, or to suffer it.

The right to have a home out of danger, and decent living conditions.

The right to go to school.

The right to play and to have recreational time.

I know how to say

NO!

The right to be protected from violence, from child abuse, and any other form of neglect or exploitation.

The right to equality and protection from all forms of discrimination.

The right to be informed, to express themselves freely, and to be listened to and respected.

Sometimes it's difficult to say no...

- because you are afraid to stand up to adults and those older than you.
- because you are scared that you, your friends, or your family may be hurt.
- because you are afraid of being rejected or made fun of.
- because you don't want to be punished, even when you are asked to do something that is bad for you.
- because you don't want to disappoint others.

You still have the right to say no!

- The right to disagree with others.
- The right to refuse to do something that you feel is inappropriate.
- The right to not accept what is being offered.

Knowing how to say no is important for your growth and development.

The right to have a kind and loving family life.

FOR LES ARÈNES
Book Design Seymourina Cruse and Victoria Scoffier
Artistic Direction Mélina Bourgoin
Editors Audrey Guillemet and Isabelle Paccalet
Maps Young Mi Dino Pereira and Lucille Dugast
Photogravure Axiome
Foreign Rights BAM Literary Agency and The Picture Book Agency

FOR DK
Editor Vicky Armstrong
Project Art Editor Jon Hall
Designer Ray Bryant
Cover Design Katherine Radcliffe
Production Editor Marc Staples
Senior Production Controller Louise Daly
Senior Commissioning Editor Katy Flint
Managing Art Editor Vicky Short
Publishing Director Mark Searle

The publisher would like to thank the following for their kind permission to reproduce their photographs: **169 Dreamstime.com:** Maksim Grebeshkov (cr).

First American Edition, 2023
Published in the United States by DK Publishing,
1745 Brodway, 20th Floor, New York, NY 10019

Page design copyright © 2023 Dorling Kindersley Limited
© Les Arènes, 2023

DK, a Division of Penguin Random House LLC
23 24 25 26 27 10 9 8 7 6 5 4 3 2 1
001–336939–Aug/23

A catalog record for this book is available from the Library of Congress
ISBN: 978-0-7440-8571-6

DK books are available at special discounts when purchased in bulk for sales promotions, premiums, fundraising, or educational use. For details, contact: DK Publishing Special Markets, 1745 Broadway, 20th Floor, New York, NY 10019
SpecialSales@dk.com

Printed and bound in China

For the curious
www.dk.com

This book was made with Forest Stewardship Council™ certified paper – one small step in DK's commitment to a sustainable future.
For more information go to www.dk.com/our-green-pledge